The world ocean. The vast mid-oceanic ridge winds its way for 40,000 miles through all three branches of the world ocean. The shorter but deeper oceanic trenches are shown here as shaded rectangles.

Must the
Seas Die?

Must the Seas Die?

Colin Moorcraft

Gambit
Boston
1973

Preface vii

Preface

For the last five years the industrialized nations of the world have been experiencing a remarkable explosion of environmental awareness. Many factors may be involved in this dramatic growth in concern, the most obvious stimulant being the increasing impact of industry on our way of life and on our environment. As the scale of industry increases so does the scale of its accidents and of the damage which its routine activities cause to living systems. The destruction of supertankers, the damage to recreational environments and the poisoning of people by chemical effluents are so effectively publicized that even those not directly involved start to worry.

Increased environmental degradation is not of itself an adequate explanation for the flowering of the environment movement. A further factor must be a straightforward increase in positive interest in the living world. This expresses itself not in attacks against industrial adventures but in statistics showing a marked increase in recreational activities involving natural and pseudo-natural environments (for example, boating, fishing and golf). The advertising industry, which often acts as a reliable indicator of the aspirations of consumer societies, places much more emphasis on "naturalness" than it did a few years ago. Many products (even cars) are paraded for their "natural" qualities and displayed in natural settings.

The growth of awareness is now so strong that it is in many ways self-sustaining. The more we care about the environment the more we want to know about how it works and about the ways in which man affects those workings. The more we find out the more worried we get—and so on.

The roots of the current environmental action movement lie in a multiplicity of local small-scale operations. Communities began to wonder if they had not reaped sufficient of the benefits of industrial society to call for a small halt. People who were financially secure and confident of their potential social significance began to question the plans of industrialists in Europe and North America. Power stations, oil refineries and other industrial developments were blocked in areas where legal expertise existed or could be bought.

The movement has spread in many directions from this essentially "conservationist" base. Different people are attacking different targets for different reasons. In West Germany, Britain and the United States many poorer communities have come to realize that the appalling environmental conditions they often have to tolerate are not inevitable and that change is possible. Attention has widened to a much broader critique of a society based on an ever-expanding economy and an ever-expanding industrial production.

The consumer movement has focused its attentions on the very fruits of industry and revealed far more than tales of environmental skullduggery (shocking as many of these are). It has gone on to document the deceptiveness of advertising, the dangers of certain products to life and limb, the inefficiency of other products (and their wastefulness of material resources) and the greed underlying the economics of consumption. In the United States the consumer movement has also taken a look at governmental institutions to make them responsive to public concerns. Similar movements have recently been established in Japan, Great Britain, Sweden and other European countries.

This expansion of scope has reached its logical conclusion in the attempts now being made to understand and cope with the degradation of the environment on a global scale. There has been much academic debate about the underlying causes of the sudden increase in pollution in the last few decades. While it is clear that it must be due in part to industrial expansion and to changes in industrial processes (involving increased consumption of resources and a switch from natural to synthetic materials) it is also clear that the world's rapidly expanding population must be a factor of some significance.

The most ambitious project undertaken to gain an understanding of the environmental and other factors limiting human growth on a global scale was that initiated by the Club of Rome. This involved the construction of a computer model based on explicit assumptions about pollution, industrial growth, food production, depletion of resources and population growth. Extrapolations from existing data were made to discover what might happen if these phenomena grew in certain ways (some of these conclusions will be briefly described later in this book). So far the project has restricted itself to analysis of our predicament. The next step is bound to be a grand plan for the management of the global environment and its resources.

Meanwhile the majority of the world's population continues to live in dire conditions and is more concerned with day-to-day issues of survival. It is only recently that the environmental movement has started to pay any considerable attention to the plight of the developing countries and of the poor in developed countries. It is becoming clear that any restructuring of industry must take these people's interests and rights into account. Other gaps created by the rapid growth of environmental awareness are also beginning to be filled. Alternative sources of energy are being investigated; new smaller-scale techniques are being devised to achieve some of the benefits of industrial technology without its undesirable social and environmental effects;

attempts are being made to escape from the pharmaceutical syndrome of modern medicine.

This book is concerned with one of the biggest gaps: awareness of the decline of marine life. It is incredible that so little attention has been paid to the enormous damage we have done to life in the seas. This is arguably our greatest environmental blunder and yet it is one that is rarely mentioned. This silence is perhaps indicative of the attitudes which led us to harm it so greatly. We have been so preoccupied with the instances of air and water pollution on our doorstep that we have neglected to consider the ultimate consequences of these forms of pollution when they reach the sea—as they nearly always do (rivers run into the seas and rain carries atmospheric pollutants into them). It could well be that marine pollution is a much more critical problem than any other form of environmental assault.

Alarm

1

For the past five years much public attention has been paid to the degradation of the environment. While much of this concern has centered on essentially local issues there is a growing awareness that the processes involved are global in scale. The biggest, most significant changes are probably those which have occurred in the vast expanses of the world's oceans and seas, yet it is these changes which have received the least attention. The silence is broken by occasional extraordinarily gloomy forecasts of the imminent destruction of all sea life. Some of the earliest of these emanated from Dr. Paul Ehrlich, a charismatic American professor of biology. In an article entitled "Eco-Catastrophe!" he painted a grim picture of gradual but rapid environmental decline. The centerpiece of his scenario is the decline of sea life:

> It was clear by 1975 that the entire ecology of plankton, the tiny animals which eat the phyto-plankton [microscopic plants] community led inevitably to changes in the community of zoo-plankton, the tiny animals which eat the phyto-plankton. These changes were passed on up the chains of life in the oceans to the herring,

plaice, cod and tuna. As the diversity of life in the ocean diminished, its stability also decreased . . . The end of the ocean came late in the summer of 1979 and it came even more rapidly than the biologists had expected. There had been signs for more than a decade . . .

In 1969, the same year as this prediction was made, the annual world fish catch actually declined for the first time in twenty-five years—despite increased investment in the fishing industry and the growing technological advancement of its equipment.

Those who find Ehrlich's warnings in general too frequent and too strident may attach more credibility to some of the more restrained but equally alarming testimonies made in November 1971 to meetings of the United States Senate Subcommittee on Oceans and the Atmosphere. Professor Barry Commoner warned that "The oceans have become the world's sink and the death of the oceans will be the death of us all." In a previous testimony the Norwegian anthropologist, explorer and author Thor Heyerdahl had reported on oil pollution he had observed in the remotest stretches of the mid-Atlantic during the voyages of his two papyrus craft, Ra I and Ra II, from Africa to tropical America. It was not a question of isolated slicks but rather of collections of tarry globules dispersed throughout the ocean for hundreds of square miles: "drifting oil clots were observed 40 out of the 57 days it took Ra II to cross the Atlantic." Heyerdahl compared these observations with his voyage across the Pacific in the Kon-Tiki, two decades earlier, when no signs of human pollution were seen.

Commandant Jacques-Yves Cousteau, the French pioneer of underwater exploration, spoke from an impressive array of experience. He probably has more firsthand experience of life in the seas than any other man alive. He opened his testimony as follows:

The sea is threatened. We are facing the destruction of the ocean by pollution and by other causes.
My role in this gigantic enterprise is only that of a witness, a

modest witness, who has only one valuable thing to testify about and it is, I think, a unique quality of experience—underwater searching with companions for more than thirty years.

We believe that the damage done to the ocean in the last twenty years is somewhere between 30 percent and 50 percent, which is a frightening figure. And this damage carries on at very high speed—to the Indian Ocean, to the Red Sea, to the Mediterranean, to the Atlantic. Our latest observations in the Pacific Ocean, in Micronesia and New Caledonia and in the Fiji Islands, are even more frightening.

These messages have one thing in common: behind the increasingly frequent and spectacular local instances of marine pollution lies a far more insidious and worrying global pattern of slow decline. This decline is not seen as a vague distant threat, unlike many other better publicized environmental depredations, but as a process which is already well under way and might even have already proceeded so far that it will be difficult or impossible to stop.

So far no marine biologist has contradicted the assertion that the seas are in decline. On the contrary, more and more are coming to express serious concern as they receive worse and worse evidence. Little of this concern has leaked through to the media and thereby expressed itself as a solid body of opinion; nonetheless decisionmakers the world over have spent the last two years getting increasingly concerned, and hardly a week goes by without an international conference being held on some aspect of the marine environment. Newspapers may be unable to carry front-page banner headlines about phytoplankton but governmental and intergovernmental agencies have access to scientists who can attempt to communicate to them about such important matters. Even when the agencies understand the complexities of the situation they are faced with, action is difficult. The marine crisis is simply one aspect of a much wider single eco-crisis. Much marine pollution starts life as atmospheric pollution or pollution of surface waters on land and is difficult to trace; control is hindered by the complex international legal structure which regulates marine affairs; lack of basic information makes it difficult to formulate scientifically convincing grounds for restrictive controls. A further irony is that the strengthening of antipollution measures on land seems to be increasing the load on the seas. It does appear, however, that the opinion is gaining ground in the international agencies that the decline of marine life could be the most critical expression of the eco-crisis. Furthermore, measures which solved this problem would of necessity go a long way to solving other major environmental problems.

Whatever the opinion of some scientists, explorers and politicians, it might seem strange that such a gigantic, subtly controlled system as the ocean could be adversely affected by the activities of man. How could he possibly undo the work of 3,000 million years in a few decades? One clue lies in man's attitude to the size of the ocean. To him it is so big as to be, in practical terms, infinite. He has treated it as an infinite source of food and as an infinite sink for his wastes. He is now discovering that the seas are finite after all. If too many individuals from any one species are taken out of the seas there comes a point where breeding cannot keep pace and the population of that species crashes: this in turn upsets the balance of those species which it eats and which eat it. When too much of the wrong sort of materials is poured into the oceans the constancy of the marine environment, which is essential to marine life, is upset.

Because the world ocean is not only the recipient of directly dumped pollutants but is also the ultimate sink for much atmospheric and fresh water pollutants, it collects staggering quantities of them. There is so much lead, for example, in the seas in their natural state that one might not expect the occasional human releases of a little more to have much effect. Yet we now know that the cumulative effect of man's releases has been sufficient at least to double the amount of lead in the marine environment all over the planet.

As well as increasing the quantities of naturally occurring elements we are further upsetting the stability of the chemical composition of the seas by introducing entirely new substances into them. Something in the order of half a million substances are released by industry into the global environment; most of these find their way to the ocean and many of them cause problems when they arrive. Marine life is equipped to break down and use a wide range of chemical compounds but we have stretched it well beyond its limits. Unfortunately it is often the case that while marine life cannot break down an alien substance, the reverse can happen—and the results are usually both adverse and hard to detect. More damage can be done to a species and to an ecosystem by a substance which slows down or distorts its life processes than by one which kills outright.

If individual compounds can be dangerous, their combined effects can be positively scaring and nightmarish for the scientist to unravel. The damage done by these compounds is heightened by the fact that some of them can survive in the ocean for hundreds and thousands of years, whereas in surface waters on land they would be removed in a matter of years, or decades at the most. The ocean is geared to relaxed cycles of thousands of years—not to the frenetic pace of human development. The nature of marine life is a further aggravating factor. Marine organisms are not only accustomed to a far more stable environment than other organisms: they are also vulnerable because of their porosity (which allows damaging substances to be absorbed into them) and because of the very small size of most of them.

Our knowledge of the decline of the marine ecosystem is strictly limited by our lack of knowledge of it in its pristine state. The International Biological Programme (IBP) is one of the biggest hopes that global surveys of ecosystems, including the marine ecosystem, might be made before it is too late. It is severely hampered by a lack of adequately trained researchers and by the hard-headedness of governments with economic problems that concern them more than environmental problems. The American government, for example, willingly pays out well over 4,000 million dollars on nonmilitary space projects but finds itself unable to pay up one-half of 1 percent of that amount for IBP. It is ironic that the same government spends thousands of millions of dollars on oceanographic research of a depressingly limited nature—a nature determined entirely by military needs. Far too many of the few oceanographers and marine biologists available are working on military projects with little value to the real problems that face us in the seas. Meanwhile we will have to accept that we know very little about the detailed causes of the decline of the marine ecosystem and that the tragic knowledge of its effects is our only compensation.

Before investigating in detail the evidence for allegations that marine life is in serious decline, it would be as well to ask the callous question: so what?

In the immediate future our principal dependence on sea life is as a source of food. From the earliest of times man has been a fisheater; archaeologists have found fishbones and discarded shells among the remains of our most primitive ancestors. Since then we have improved our hunting methods dramatically and our population has also increased spectacularly. The present world population is just over 3,500 million and its rate of increase is 1.8 percent annually, so that it doubles every thirty to forty years. By the year 2000 world population will probably be at least 6,000 million. Official projections of the United Nation's Food and Agriculture Organization for the coming decade show that population growth threatens to outstrip growth in food production so that there may be as many hungry and poorly fed people in 1980 as there are today.

In the two decades from 1948 to 1967 the world fish catch grew at a considerably faster rate than both world population and agricultural food production. (The world fish catch has doubled twice in the past twenty-five years.) In theory agricultural production could increase at a greater rate than it is doing, since much potential arable land is not being used, land is being wasted on nonfood crops, and low-yielding unproductive crops are widely grown. In practice social and economic realities act as a brake, and climate acts as a capricious reverse gear: two bad seasons in 1965 and 1966 canceled out the progress of a decade in the developing countries.

The world fish catch represents only a few percent of the world's calorie intake (calories are a measure of the energy content of food) but its main value is as a source of protein. Half the world's population gets half its protein from fish. The nutritional value of fish is in most ways equal to, or greater than, that of meat. Plankton-eating fish have a considerably higher proportion of protein in their flesh than lean meat. Saltwater fish are also the only animals with backbones that contain all the earth's minerals in digestible form, and many essential vitamins are found in relatively large quantities in some fish. In addition to these nutritional properties, fish need little fuel for cooking and are easily digested. On the other hand they perish more easily than meat and need to be preserved if they are to be transported over any long distance or if they are to be stored for any period of time.

When one considers the amount of land saved by extracting protein from the seas it becomes readily apparent that seafish are essential to human survival and can only become more so. If a fish-eating country such as Japan were forced to abandon fish as a source of protein, it would require double its total land area to produce land-based animal proteins. Even the U.S.A. would feel the squeeze. Americans eat very little fish but they feed their poultry, pigs and other livestock on fishmeal. Despite their agricultural surplus they would have to increase dairy production by 22 percent if they replaced fishmeal with skim milk. These sums will get even more dramatic as populations increase and as farm land is swallowed up by industries and by cities.

Fishing not only supplies vital protein and eases pressure on already overstrained land-based agriculture, it also employs large numbers of men and makes money. Over 200 nations are engaged in fishing the seas. In Japan alone more than 2 million people derive their living from fishing and some small countries survive almost entirely on fishing. In Iceland, for example, 21 percent of the entire labor force is engaged in fishing and fish processing. The current retail value of the world catch is estimated to be about 10,000 million pounds.

It is in the developing countries that fish protein is most needed and will become even more vital. The population explosion is most marked in those countries with the lowest per-capita food production and income. They are fast outstripping the capacity of their soil to support them and in the space of a generation have switched from being net grain exporters to being importers of more than 30 million tons of grain a year. In the last decade the developing countries' share of world trade has fallen from 27 to 17 percent so it is becoming increasingly difficult for them to afford to import food. The net result of these pressures is starvation, disease and misery on a terrible scale. The implications of widespread hunger are many. Resistance to disease, the ability to work and most other human capabilities are all lowered. Starvation during infancy has been found to retard mental development. The most important aspect of starvation in developing countries is the lack of protein. What little food that is available is often starchy (and therefore a good source of energy) but low in protein (a vital chemical building block which the body needs to take in continuously).

Severe protein deficiency leads to diseases such as kwashiorkor, which strikes children and is characterized by distension of the stomach. In some areas of Africa every child may suffer from the grotesque disease at some stage in its development. It can be fatal and when it is not it often causes permanent damage to the liver and pancreas. It is interesting to note that only fairly small amounts of daily protein are necessary to avoid deficiency. Unfortunately even a few grams is beyond the capabilities of the agriculturalists of most developing countries. In many of these countries the majority of what little protein is available is already derived from fish. This is likely to become an increasingly important source as population mushrooms.

In the developed countries population is not rising as fast, yet their consumption of fish is exploding too. This is caused by the increasing use of fishmeal to feed poultry, pigs and other livestock. Already, over half the United States poultry feed is fishmeal and the proportion is continually increasing—as is the number of birds raised annually. The conversion of fishmeal into poultry is not as inefficient as its conversion into pork but even so one cannot help feeling that the fish would be better used directly as food for humans. Apologists for the fishmeal business argue that the fish used for meal are often too small to eat. As they are often species which are eaten by man when they are bigger it might be wiser to let them grow before harvesting them. It is also possible to process small fish and fish of species not ordinarily eaten by man to obtain fish flours and fish protein concentrates (FPCs) which are a very useful dietary supplement. However, it is unlikely that the wasteful use of an increasingly large proportion of the world fish catch for fishmeal will be curtailed, as this would cause the poultry industry of the U.S.A. and Europe to collapse. It would also discomfort the pig-raising industry.

The widening gap between rich and poor is strongly reflected in the world fishery statistics. Three-quarters of the world catch is landed by fourteen of the 200 fishing nations. Of these only one, Peru, is a developing country. Peru increased its catch tenfold in a decade to become the world's leading fishing nation. It owes its position entirely to the enormous anchoveta fishery which has developed just off its coast. The inequities of global economics reassert themselves when one looks at the reason for Peru's rise to eminence and at the fate of its catch. It transpires that virtually all the catch leaves Latin America, where it is desperately needed (in the form of fish protein concentrates) to fill human stomachs, for the poultry industries of America and Europe. The Peruvian anchovy industry arose almost entirely to service the needs of the fishmeal industry.

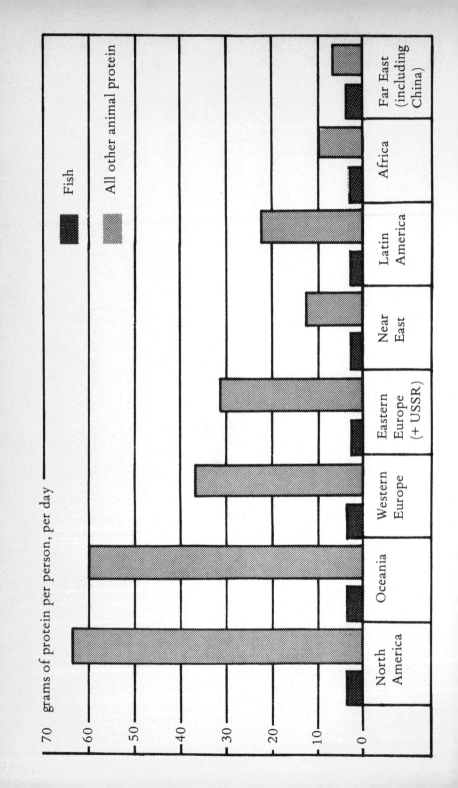

The demand for fishmeal is further reflected in statistics showing how the world catch is used. Under 10 percent of the world catch was turned into meal just before World War II. By 1967 half of it was being used in this way and the proportion is still increasing. During the same period the proportion sold fresh has declined from 53 to 31 percent but that of frozen fish has risen from almost nothing to 12 percent. This most probably reflects changes in the demands of the developed nations rather than of developing nations. It is regrettable that the developing countries, whose needs warrant consumption of at least three-quarters of the world catch, should at present account for the consumption of a meager 20 percent.

The massive capital investment in the European, Russian, Japanese and American fishing industries will only serve to increase existing inequities. Fish processing plants are at present working under capacity. In order to satisfy their demands more fish will inevitably have to be caught and diverted from more deserving uses. Fishing technology is a growth technology. Ever more sensitive electronic gadgets are being marketed to detect fish. Net mesh sizes are decreasing. Nets themselves are on the way out: fishing technocrats are now talking of electronic guidance systems to attract fish and guide them towards enormous suction pumps which would suck them onboard. Poorer nations will find it increasingly difficult to compete on these terms. They may even find that untapped or little worked fisheries off their coasts will be tapped by richer nations who have squeezed their own fisheries dry.

In the unlikely event of a world revolution on food distribution next week we would still need to extract enormous quantities of protein from the seas. The Food and Agriculture Organization (FAO) of the United Nations has calculated that the protein needs of the Far East alone would require a catch of more than 82 million tons by the year 2000 (the 1970 world catch—excluding China—was 69.3 million tons). At one time 80 million tons was regarded as the limit for the annual world catch. At present 120 million tons seems a more popular figure. Either way we are going to have to start to use the world catch more intelligently if we are sincere in our wishes to reduce protein malnutrition. One way would be to make more effective use of that part of the catch which is destined for the dinner plate. Current habits lead to the wastage of more than half of the whole fish before it reaches the plate. Fish flours and fish protein concentrates make use of the entire fish and are quite palatable. The use of fish flour in Senegal reduced infant mortality by two-thirds. It would also make sense if aid given to developing countries were directed towards the strengthening of indigenous fishing industries. Many tropical fisheries are untapped or underused and they could be exploited by using labor-intensive methods appropriate to the local countries, as opposed to the customary capital-intensive fantasies of aid donors. The simple introduction of outboard motors to a traditional sail-based industry can make a very significant difference and allow local fishermen to compete with the boats of distant richer nations.

Man's ever-increasing need for protein will cause him to look beyond the species he currently uses as seafood. A logical development would be to move down the food chains, as the seas support a greater mass of life at the lower levels. The plankton at the very bottom of the food chain are unlikely to be tapped directly as an excessive amount of energy is needed to filter the immense volumes of water necessary to obtain very small quantities of food. It is possible, however, that we will soon be able to harvest on a large scale shrimp-like animals known as "krill." These are found in abundance in the Antarctic seas and are big enough (half an inch to two inches long) to make their collection economically feasible. Russian and Japanese boats are already collecting krill in small quantities and a total world catch of 30 million tons (5 million of which would be protein) is expected. Further up the food chain, we could start to use a few more of the 20,000 species of fish which inhabit the world ocean, especially those which feed exclusively on microscopic plants—the phytoplankton. We might even consider adding to our hunting skills the skills of the sea farmer. The farming of shellfish is an exceptionally efficient way of producing protein. Some existing Spanish mussel beds yield an annual weight, excluding shells, of 300,000 kilograms per hectare (for comparison, the average yield of trawled fishes in continental shelf water is twenty-five to seventy-five kilograms per hectare). Clearly we will find it more and more necessary to conserve all species of marine life for potential future use as food and keep the marine environment stable so as to enable sea farming to expand in the future.

As land resources become more depleted and uneconomic to use, industry is starting to look to the seas and to life in them for some of its future resources. Fish oil is already an important raw material for industry. It is used in the manufacture of soap, candles, paints, waterproofing liquids, varnishes and linoleum. Seaweeds, which have long been used for food, are a source of alginates which can be used in many ways by the chemical industry (particularly in the manufacture of plastics). Extensive research is being conducted by the pharmaceutical industry to detect new sources of medical materials in marine organisms and so far they have found a few good antibiotics and other materials.

As well as using individual species as resources for our immediate well-being, we will become more dependent on the health of the ecosystem as a whole, as more and more people come to live in coastal regions and to use the sea for recreation. Recent UN statistics show a world-wide process of rapid urbanization. A fifth of the world's population lives in the world's ten most populous cities: Tokyo, New York, London, Moscow, Shanghai, Bombay, Sao Paulo, Rio de Janeiro and Peking. All of them except Moscow are situated on the coast, as are most other large cities. A United States government report forecasts that 50 percent of the U.S. population will be living within a hundred miles of the seashore and the Great Lakes by the year 2000. Future coastal populations will not want their health put at hazard by an unhealthy marine ecosystem—which would be accompanied by widespread decomposition of dead matter on beaches and in shallow waters. Those who spend their holidays by the sea or use it for sports (such as swimming, diving, fishing and sailing) would also be put at risk by a dying ocean. According to the American report just cited, 150 to 200 million people will be using American beaches by the end of the century. At present 30 million of them swim in the ocean, 11 million are salt-water sports fishermen and eight million go boating. The figures for other developed countries are, proportionately, equally large.

The health of the entire marine ecosystem and the continued stability of the entire marine environment are equally critical in the long-term. If the delicate, interconnected global cycles of energy and materials are disrupted, man will indubitably succeed in making his home planet uninhabitable for himself, and probably for all other forms of life. We still know very little about these cycles and there is a lively scientific debate about the consequences of the possible death of the marine ecosystem. It is pointed out that the majority of the atmosphere's oxygen is replenished by the marine phytoplankton and that they are also the biggest remover of carbon dioxide from the atmosphere. The first effects of any change in the balance of oxygen and carbon dioxide in the atmosphere would probably be seen in the climate. The precise changes are disputed: some see another ice age, others see a raising of the world's temperature and the melting of the ice caps. Ultimately, in one or two thousand years, the air would perhaps become unbreathable for man and other animals. Whatever the details, there can be no disputing that marine life is a critically important element of the cyclic processes which occur on the surface of our planet and that to disrupt it seriously is to disrupt the cycles equally seriously.

It can be seen that any threat to the world ocean and the life within it is also a major threat to the immediate and long-term survival of man. It could well be that the decline of the marine ecosystem is the most critical environmental threat facing mankind.

The World Ocean

2

It is often conjectured that a passing spaceman, seeing Earth for the first time, might well name it the Water Planet. His view of the surface would be largely impeded by clouds of water vapor, and through the gaps between these clouds he would catch glimpses of immense bodies of water and some scattered masses of land bearing the scars of erosion by water.

Closer examination would reveal that the bodies of water, which we call oceans and seas, interconnect to form what is, in effect, a world ocean. This single mass of water encircles the globe and determines much of the physical and chemical processes which occur on it.

The world ocean consists of 330,000 cubic miles of sea water which covers most of the planet, leaving only 29 percent of the surface to the continental land masses. If its floors were leveled it would have a depth of 11,600 feet, whereas the continents, if similarly leveled, would only rise to a height of 2780 feet.

The features of the basin which contains this enormous mass of water are equally impressive in their dimensions. The margins of the basin are largely occupied by continental shelves—extensive flat areas stretching out from the adjacent land masses which were submerged by a shallow layer of sea water when enormous sheets of ice melted at the ends of previous ice ages. Their gradient is very gentle, averaging about one in one thousand; their depth is usually less than 600 feet and they can be as wide as 750 miles in the Arctic.

The continental shelves give way to tall steep continental slopes which plunge down to the floor of the ocean basin. The slopes are the planet's longest, highest escarpments, averaging 12,000 feet in height but reaching an incredible 30,000 feet in some places. The bases of most continental slopes give way to stretches of sea bed which climb again gently to form continental rises. In some areas, parallel to island chains or to nearby continental mountain ranges, the continental slope does not rise at its base but, instead, drops into a series of extraordinarily long, deep and narrow trenches. One of these, the Tonga-Kermadec Trench, is seven times as deep as the Grand Canyon, five miles wide and almost completely straight. The deepest trench is the Philippines Trench which at one point descends to a depth of 37,782 feet.

Beyond the rises and trenches of the continental margins lie the immense ocean basin floors which occupy over one-third of the planet's surface. These consist largely of plains as flat as the continental shelves and of rolling hills 300 to 1,200 feet high. In a few places, much taller rises and ridges jut up from the ocean basin floor and pierce the surface, creating oceanic islands such as Tristan da Cunha and the Bermuda Islands. A vast tonnage of sediment is spread across large areas of the abyssal plains and hills and the continental shelves, forming layers as much as 12,000 feet thick.

The most remarkable oceanic feature is perhaps the Mid-Oceanic Ridge. This is a first-order global feature comparable in scale to the continents and to the world ocean itself. It is surprising that its enormous extent has only recently been appreciated by man and that he has yet to explore it in any detail. It is a continuous submerged mountain chain that worms its way for 40,000 miles along the middle of the world ocean's three major branches (the Pacific, Atlantic and Indian Oceans) and is equal in area to all of the continents. Its height above the surrounding ocean basin floor varies from one to 10,000 feet and it is rarely less than 700 miles wide. A deep, wide trench runs all the way along its crest. In the mid-Atlantic the trench has an average depth of 6,000 feet and is from eight to thirty miles across (the Grand Canyon's depth is four thousand feet and its width varies from four to eighteen miles).

However impressive the dimensions of the Water Planet's ocean might be to a passing spaceman, its chemical and physical properties could not fail to impress him to a far greater extent. These properties are extremely complex, yet they have remained virtually constant for hundreds of millions of years —despite many major geological and climatic changes which have occurred during the same period. Such constancy is dependent on extremely subtle controls which allow the ocean to respond flexibly to external changes and to balance its own internal processes.

The world ocean is enormously active, all the time absorbing heat energy from the sun and mechanical energy from the winds; breathing in carbon dioxide and other gases from the atmosphere; gulping up large quantities of a wide variety of materials brought to it by rivers, rain, snow and the melting of polar ice; moving continuously and thus thoroughly mixing the materials it receives as well as distributing the sun's heat energy; releasing heat to the atmosphere; breathing out oxygen and other gases; eliminating excess materials (by, for example, sedimentation and the formation of sedimentary rocks). Faced with this diverse, peculiarly stable, wonderfully co-ordinated web of activities our spaceman might well look upon the world ocean as more than a puddle of spectacular dimensions. He might see it as a single gargantuan living organism and would perhaps rename our planet the Living-Water Planet.

One of the most distinctive properties of the world ocean is its chemical composition. Sea water is exceptionally rich chemically containing in solution almost every known element. Its richness is due both to the great ability of water to dissolve chemicals (an ability which is not exceeded by any other liquid) and to the very wide range of chemical material which enters it. The world ocean receives the river-borne products of the erosion of the many different rocks of the continents and absorbs further geologically derived materials dissolved in rain and snow and released by melting polar ice. Although the types of material which enter it vary considerably from place to place (due, for example, to variations in the amount of rainfall falling on a given area of ocean or to the sort of rocks which rivers drain), the relative proportions of sea water's many constituents are found to be the same everywhere in the world ocean.

Even more surprising is the discovery by geologists that the relative proportions have probably been almost constant for the past 600 million years. This is particularly puzzling when one thinks of the many enormous chemical changes which have occurred on land in the same period, and we still do not fully understand the elaborate controls which maintain sea water's rich composition. The electronic balance of the differently charged elements is probably an important factor and could be linked to the processes of sedimentation which eliminate excess materials. Another key factor is the continuous motion of every single particle of sea water. Man has known for a long time about the currents which move the surface waters of the world ocean but recently he has started to discover that even the deepest waters, hitherto considered to be static and stagnant, are moved by powerful currents. The net effect of this perpetual motion is to mix chemicals thoroughly, like a global slow-motion cocktail shaker.

Oceanic motion is also closely linked to sea water's important physical properties—especially its thermal properties. Sea water has a capacity to store heat exceeded only by liquid ammonia, and one implication of this capacity is that it requires a comparatively enormous quantity of heat to raise the temperature of the ocean by the smallest amount. Consequently the temperature of the sea water in any one locality changes much more slowly than that of the atmosphere above it. It is estimated that a 1 percent increase in the quantity of solar energy reaching earth would raise the atmospheric temperature by 15 degrees centigrade, while it would raise the world oceanic temperature by a mere 0.01 degrees.

The temperature of the ocean is so constant that it acts as a considerable stabilizing influence on the temperature of the atmosphere and the continental land masses—hence the world ocean's frequent description as the "global thermostat." The thermostat is made even more effective by cold polar waters which sink and flow to the equatorial regions. If it were not for the seas of our planet, its continents would experience temperatures similar to those on the surface of the moon.

Man's view of the major surface feature of his home planet differs considerably from what might be expected of the extraterrestrial traveler. Our view is that of a land-based observer whose conception of the world ocean has arisen piecemeal from our use of it for military purposes, for transportation, as a source of food and as a sink for wastes. It was only comparatively recently that we deduced that the seas interconnect to form a single world ocean which encircles all the land masses on which we live. Our current picture of the world ocean is a jigsaw with many missing bits and with many bits carrying only the scantest information, and there are still many aspects of it about which we have little or no knowledge.

One of these is marine life. Few of us see the world ocean as a single gargantuan living organism. We see it as a very large mass of nonliving sea water containing a relatively small mass of small, separate, living organisms. For us a living organism is an entity like ourselves: any small but highly structured bundle of matter and energy that struggles to maintain itself, grows, reproduces and dies. This emphasis on the separation of individuals from each other and from their environment may stem from the constraints of early biology which was largely concerned with classification and hence with the investigation of characteristics which distinguish living things from each other. Subsequent biologists investigated the interlinked global cycles in which matter and energy flow within organisms, between different organisms, and between organisms and their environment. This emphasis on unity and interconnectedness, rather than separation, is slowly establishing a new scientific attitude to life. Early biology attempted, for example, to determine the form of the organ where a plant stored water so that it became possible to distinguish that plant from others. Later work was able to proceed from this useful, but static, basis to build up a dynamic model of the processes whereby water enters the plant, moves within it to the storage organ and finally makes its way out again. Even this is only part of the story. Once it leaves the plant, the water enters the atmosphere, is carried away, becomes part of a cloud, falls as rain over the sea, is carried by a strong current to a distant part of the planet, evaporates to reenter the atmosphere, falls as rain over land, is absorbed from the land by a plant—and so on. This is an example of just one global cycle, the hydrological cycle.

Despite their interconnectedness, the similarity in chemical composition of all living organisms is still surprising. It is even more surprising that their composition is similar to that of sea water. Even man, who sometimes likes to think of himself as a superior life form, carries within his body a portable ocean. Not only are blood plasma and other bodily fluids peculiarly similar to brackish sea water, but the overall composition of the body is also like that of the seas. Each of us starts life as a foetus buoyed up in amniotic fluid, a warm mass of dilute sea water-like liquid that maintains a wet, warm, chemically rich environment of outstanding constancy. Now some biologists are turning the tables by suggesting not that we each contain a portable ocean but that the ocean contains a continuously moving bloodstream—in the form of sea water. They argue that sea water is a biological fluid performing much the same functions as blood plasma. It provides a constant environment and acts as a transport medium for nutrients, waste products, dissolved gases and heat. Nonetheless marine biology is still influenced by its origins. This book will largely be a chronicle of the consequences of our failure to see the entire world ocean as a finite, integrated whole.

Whatever biological approach one takes, it becomes clear that the world ocean has been a dominant influence in the development of life on our planet. The shared chemical composition of sea water and living organisms is no coincidence, for it is thought that life originated in the seas over 3,000 million years ago.

Three of the four major forms of life appear to have developed there very rapidly. These were the Monera, Protista and Metazoa. The Monera are primitive one-cell organisms with a very simple internal structure. They exist today as bacteria and blue-green algae. The Protista have the ability to convert the sun's energy into chemical energy (an extremely important process known as photosynthesis); they group together to form multicellular organisms and have more complex cells. They can be seen now as seaweeds, fungi, slime moulds and protozoa. They could be loosely described as plants just as early representatives of the third group, the Metazoa, could be called animals. The Metazoa were as complex as the Protista but could not photosynthesize and therefore had to obtain energy in other ways—usually by eating Protista or each other. Their descendants include the sponges and all animal life.

The fourth major division of life, the Metaphyta, did not make its appearance until much later—a mere 350 million years ago. Like the other divisions, it is thought to have originated in the seas (possible from seaweed-like Protista living near the seashore). Existing descendants include all the mosses, ferns, flowering plants and trees.

The Metaphyta soon evolved in such a way that some

species were able to leave the seas and colonize the land. They were shortly followed by some animal species of the Metazoa. It is interesting that for the great majority of its history life has been a specifically marine phenomenon but that when the transition to land was made it required only slight modifications. Even now land life is little more than modified sea life and many animals have successfully returned to the seas. Man has managed to get dogs and hamsters to breathe underwater. One day he may himself be able to swim in sea water without any artificial breathing apparatus, thanks to careful surgical modifications to his lungs.

Marine life is still the most abundant form of life on our planet. The basis of all marine life is plant life as it is this which taps solar energy by photosynthesis and converts it to the chemical energy which fuels all other forms of life. Most marine plants are considerably smaller than land plants—often microscopic—and float freely at the mercy of the currents, tides and other motions of the seas. These free-floating plants are collectively known as the phytoplankton and live in surface waters where they are bathed in sunlight.

The phytoplankton are usually much more productive than land plants. Under favorable conditions they can double or treble their population in twenty-four hours. This high rate of production is coupled to an equally high rate of consumption. Whereas plants on land might take a year before being replaced (long-lived plants such as trees, of course, take very much longer than that) the phytoplankton grow, reproduce and die as food for another organism in the space of a few days. Consequently, while there may not be an enormous mass of phytoplankton around at any one time, the amount produced over any lengthy period is enormous. It is estimated that the weight of phytoplankton at any single moment constitutes only 0.01 percent of the total weight of plant material on earth. Yet this minuscule proportion is thought to account for 40 percent, by weight, of the total weight of plant material produced on earth during the course of a year. Clearly the phytoplankton are critically significant, if little appreciated, forms of life. We shall see later that they may also be its Achilles heel.

The microscopic phytoplankton are by no means the only plants in the seas. The sun-bathed sea floors of coastal areas often have forests of seaweeds attached to them, and these too are extremely productive plants. Although they only cover a meager 0.1 percent of the total surface area of the sea they contribute a significant percentage to the annual productivity of all marine plants. Various calculations suggest that marine plants are probably collectively responsible for well over half (perhaps as much as 80 percent) of the total annual productivity of all the plants of our planet.

As the world ocean occupies over two-thirds of the world's surface and provides, throughout its mass, a physically and chemically stable environment with all the chemical elements necessary for growth, it might seem natural that it should be responsible for so much plant productivity. Yet many marine biologists describe the open ocean as an infertile "biological desert," saying that as much as 90 percent of the world ocean is almost bereft of life. This apparent disparity arises from the fact that the nutrients, although present in all the necessary forms, occur in very low concentrations. Take nitrogen, for example. This element, together with phosphorus, is essential for plant growth and its presence has a marked effect on plant productivity. It can be found in fertile soil on land in concentrations up to 0.5 percent but in fertile sea water it would be unlikely to exceed 0.00005 percent. Such considerations serve to emphasise the amazing productivity of those areas of the seas where life does occur.

The vast quantities of energy and materials harnessed by the marine plants support a sizable population of consumer organisms. According to Russian calculations, four-fifths, by weight, of the world's animals are to be found in the ocean. These include sponges, shellfish and mammals.

Many marine animals have far more complex life cycles

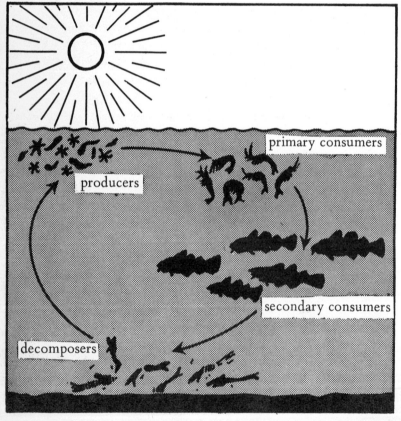

The normal cycle of marine life

than land animals and pass through various distinct larval stages. Most start life as microscopic, free-floating organisms —known collectively as zooplankton. The zooplankton feed directly on the phytoplankton (and on each other) and this conversion of plant matter into animal matter is the first link in the food chain. Like all the other links, it is far from efficient: it takes roughly ten pounds of phytoplankton to produce one pound of zooplankton. As the food chains of the seas are frequently longer than those on land (often having five steps, ending up with big carnivorous fish and predatory animals such as the shark) there is a good deal of wastage of the original plant material. Another consequence of the successive wastages in the food chain is that animals lower down the chain occur in larger amounts than those further up. Thus plant-eating fish such as the herring are found in greater amounts than fish-eating fish such as the cod. It is also generally true that the first links in the chains occur where the plants are, in the surface layers. It is for this reason that 80 percent, by weight, of marine life is found in the top 200 meters of the ocean.

The wastes and dead bodies of the plants and their consumers drift downwards to be decomposed either en route or on arrival at the bottom. The decomposer organisms are mostly worms and microscopic creatures such as bacteria. Their job is an essential if little appreciated one: they break down wastes into their simple constituent chemical building blocks, thereby recycling them in a form which plants can use in their production processes.

As we saw earlier, sea life is far from evenly distributed, most of the world ocean is a biological desert, but in those areas where life does occur it does so with a profusion that more than compensates for its lack elsewhere. Such disparities in distribution are far from random. One overall tendency is for marine life to become less diverse but more productive as one moves from the tropics towards the poles.

In the warm, stable climate of the tropics a distinct surface layer of water is created. This layer is heated by the sun and tends to be fairly uniform in temperature throughout its mass. It is separated from the main, colder mass of oceanic water beneath it by a distinct intermediate layer known as the thermocline. The thermocline is very thin and falls quickly in temperature from its top to its bottom. It acts very much as a barrier to the two-way exchange of materials between the surface layer and the main body of the ocean. Any material, such as wastes and dead organisms, which drifts down and out of the surface layer is unlikely to be replaced. The net result is a reduction in fertility of the sun-soaked surface area and a consequent low productivity. At the same time the tropical heat promotes the processes of life essential to evolution and one finds an exciting diversity of species but few of them boast high populations. Complex communities of this sort tend to be more stable than simpler ones. In colder seas there is less of a difference between the surface temperature and the temperature of the underlying oceanic water, so thermoclines are less pronounced or even nonexistent. Vertical mixing occurs more readily and nutrients are recirculated, thus maintaining the fertility of the surface layer. Plant productivity is usually higher and surface life is abundant. On the other hand the lower, more variable temperatures are less conducive to evolutionary processes and one finds that polar life is less diverse than that in warmer zones.

A further global pattern in the distribution of sea life is that the open ocean tends to be far less productive than coastal areas. Once again the basic factor is the availability of essential nutrients. It is only in coastal areas that the world ocean's basically low concentration of nutrients is increased. This is due, in part, to the presence of materials introduced by rivers and by other runoff from the land, and also, in a few very restricted areas, to powerful upwelling currents which bring large quantities of nutrients up from the depths to the surface. These areas can be as much as six times as productive as the rest of the ocean. They have larger phytoplankton and shorter food chains. This means that a given mass of plant material can support a larger mass of consumer organisms as wastage is reduced. It is in areas such as these that man finds most of his seafood—and dumps most of his wastes.

One of the most striking coastal ecosystems (an ecosystem is a community of organisms within which producers, consumers and decomposers work in balance with each other) is the coral reef. This beautifully complex system of living things is one of the most productive ecosystems of any kind on this planet. Estuaries are also exceptionally productive and play a key role in the life of the seas, as many marine animals pass one or more of their larval stages in them before moving on to spend their adult life in a distant and possibly entirely different ecosystem. This is just one way in which separate ecosystems are interlinked. They also link trophically (that is, different members of different communities eat one another) and metabolically (when the materials produced by decomposition in one community act as nutrients for another).

Man's concept of the world ocean is slowly inching towards that which might be held by an extraterrestrial observer. The more we investigate the ocean, the greater our respect for this complex, productive, stable unity and for its intimately and subtly interconnected parts. We are also learning that we too are intimately and inseparably bound up in its workings— without life in the seas there would be no man on this planet.

Overkill

3

Ecological problems are usually caused by what we put into the environment rather than what we take out. The decline of life in the world ocean can be attributed to large scale occurrences of both activities. The ocean is man's last hunting ground and he is busy helping to ruin it by indiscriminately removing whatever he can get hold of. This may have been excusable when the illusion that seas were an infinite source of food had not been modified by scientific knowledge. We now know that not only is sea life finite but that as a consequence there is a limit to the amount we can remove without permanently depleting populations and even causing the extinction of species. Overhunting is both inexcusable and rife.

It is difficult to unravel the full impact of overhunting on current stocks of marine food organisms, as we know so little about the consequences on them of the innumerable substances human activity has introduced into the marine environment. If we look at the plight of species which were overhunted before marine pollution became apparent as a serious problem we can see how dangerous it can be. The worst examples relate

to whales and other marine mammals. Even a hundred years
ago Herman Melville was sufficiently worried by whaling to ask
"whether Leviathan can long endure so wide a chase, and so
remorseless a havoc." The answer has proved to be a
definite no.

The earliest whalers were the Basques, who hunted the Atlantic right whale in the Bay of Biscay, and the Norwegians
who hunted the same species at the same time, the tenth and
eleventh centuries. Both these fisheries established a grimly
familiar pattern of discovery followed by a rapid increase in
killing, the collapse of the stock and the "commercial extinction" of the fishery. Other species of right whale (so named
because they are the right whale to catch) in the northern
hemisphere were hunted to commercial extinction by the Scan-
dinavians, Germans, Dutch, British and anyone else who could
afford a boat and a harpoon gun. By the turn of the nineteenth century the whalers had done such a thorough job in
their hemisphere that it looked as if their industry was doomed.

Unfortunately large stocks of the rorqual whales were
found in the Antarctic and whaling started relentlessly ravag-
ing the other hemisphere. The industry was initially hindered
by the British Government which administered the waters
where the first whales were hunted and which limited the number of whale catchers as well as imposing a tax on the industry. These hindrances were cast aside when whales were
discovered in Antarctic waters beyond British jurisdiction.
Thanks to harpoons with explosive tips and to factory ships
which processed carcasses on the spot, catches escalated according to the familiar pattern. As recently as twelve years ago
65 percent of the annual world catch was taken from Antarctic
waters. It has since declined to 10 percent. During this period
of decline the yield of whale oil (now the most important commercial product of whales) was reduced to a fifth of what it
was from 2 million barrels to 400,000 in the 1969–1970 season.
The two species of right whale are now as good as extinct—
its numbers have probably been reduced to a few dozen. The

blue whale, easily the largest animal on earth, is also on the way out: its population has crashed in five years from approximately 100,000 five years ago to a few thousand today. The bowhead and humpback whales are also "commercially extinct" and reduced to very low numbers.

In 1970 the overwhelming majority of the world catch was taken by two nations: the Soviet Union (43 percent) and Japan (42 percent). The remaining 15 percent was taken by Peru (5.3 percent), South Africa (2.8 percent), Norway (2.5 percent), Canada (1.7 percent), Australia (1.4 percent), Spain (0.8 percent) and the United States (0.5 percent). Most of these were small whales such as the sei, sperm, gray and finback whales. All these species have been reduced substantially in number and will soon become commercially extinct if more stringent controls are not applied.

Despite the fact that it is putting the final touches to the digging of its own grave, the whaling industry has yet to fully grasp that uncontrolled hunting is in the long term (where long means some time after the next season) economic suicide—not to mention a tragic butchery of a beautiful and useful family of animals. An International Whaling Commission has been established to regulate the industry but it is very much a case of the poachers turning into gamekeepers. They have been extremely slow to take effective action. They set quotas to limit each nation's catch but do so by weight rather than species. The inadequacy of the quotas has done little to halt the depletion of stocks. After years of haggling, and long after it was required, the IWC has finally managed to agree that observers are necessary to curb whaling in the Antarctic. Their first season was the 1971–1972 season. Each whaling fleet has an observer assigned to it. This man is empowered to observe and to report his observations back to IWC in London but he has no power at all to suspend whaling if a fleet violates its quota. Some Japanese scientists have formed a Committee for the Protection of Whales which has produced good evidence that the Japanese government ought to control the nation's whaling industry and

The following great whales are ranked by their degree of rarity. The first group is protected. The second group is still hunted, but the herds are rapidly being depleted. Population figures are rough estimates. (By permission of the *Ecologist*)

Bowhead Double spout, great curved jaw, bonnet; Eskimo still take a few every May; its numbers are unknown.

Right (Two species) so-called because they were the "right" ones to kill in the nineteenth century; slow swimmers that floated after being harpooned; double spout, curved jaw, bonnet, barnacles; their numbers may be measured in dozens in a few remote areas.

Blue Largest animal on earth, splotchy exterior, weighs as much as 1,500 men; its numbers have dropped from perhaps 100,000 fifty years ago to a few thousand today.

Humpback Most boisterous, breaches frequently, long flippers, unexplained knobs on head, great singer; less abundant originally than the blue, its numbers today are down to a few thousand.

Gray Small rorqual; Korean stock not seen in years; following thirty years protection, the California stock has slowly recovered and now numbers 10,000–12,000.

Finback Second largest of the baleen whales, fast swimmer, asymmetrical white marking on underside that overlaps right side of jaw; its numbers are estimated at about 100,000 today against about 400,000 formerly.

Sei Third largest baleen whale, six times smaller than blue in terms of oil yield, its smaller, less numerous cousin Bryde's whale is also pursued; its members are at least one-half of what they were, 75,000 compared with perhaps 150,000.

Sperm Only great toothed whale, square-headed, corrugated body, harem groupings, diagonal spout, squid-eater, deep diver, found in all the oceans; most abundant species but its numbers are down to perhaps 250,000 from an estimated 600,000.

do all it can to strengthen the IWC. There is no news of a similar movement within the Soviet Union.

If the industry is blind to its own commercial future it is even blinder to the future of the whale and to the ecological consequences of its drastic depletion. The ecological role of whales is largely unknown as observable stocks are usually too quickly hunted to be studied rewardingly. Their diet consists almost entirely of microscopic shrimp-like krill and other forms of plankton. The whale consumes these in such large quantities that it must be an important factor in the control of the population of krill, and its removal would be expected to upset the balance between plankton and other marine organisms. There is some evidence that the depletion of Antarctic whales has affected plankton populations but it is difficult to be certain as too little is known about the other factors which control population for an assured statement to be made.

Other sea mammals are also fast being depleted. An interesting example is a small porpoise which is an inseparable companion of the yellowfin tuna. It is frequently netted with the tuna and often panics and dies in the process. Many fishermen regard the animal with affection but are not always able to save it soon enough. A quarter of a million died in 1970 as a result of the activities of American West Coast tuna fishermen. An equal number are thought to have died as the result of other nations hunting the same yellowfin tuna. No one yet knows the full subtleties of the relationship between the small porpoise and the yellowfin tuna but it is probable that their association has some purpose. It seems that the only way man will discover that purpose is by severing the bond.

Man's fishing of the seas predates even his whaling. As far back as we search we find evidence of man the fisherman. Likewise we also find early examples of fisheries collapsing, and sometimes destroying the societies based on their commercial earnings. Some of these collapses may have been partly or wholly attributable to natural causes. The collapse of the medieval Baltic herring fishery, for example, may have been caused by a naturally induced migration of the fish to new feeding grounds. It was certainly a blow to the Hansa merchants who profited considerably from the herring and who may well have speeded its collapse by encouraging overfishing.

Overfishing first became a serious problem in the early decades of this century, just before marine pollution started to further complicate the picture. The first indications of wide-scale overfishing were obtained in the North Sea in a series of experiments conducted before the first world war. It was noticed that the average size of the plaice being caught was getting smaller and smaller and that larger fish were being removed at a greater rate than the smaller fish could replace them (this pattern was similar to that which was found in whales). Scientists attached tags to some of the fish and released them. As much as 70 percent were recaught by fishermen in the following year, suggesting that at least that proportion of the total stock was being removed each year. Yields as high as that could not be sustained for long. The nations which fished the North Sea at that time discussed various suggestions for restoring stocks but could not agree how to do it. Their deliberations were interrupted by the first world war—which quickly solved the problem by turning the North Sea into a battle zone too dangerous to fish. After the war the fishermen went about their business again and found that both the overall size of their catch and the sizes of individual fish had increased considerably during the nonfishing period. By the end of the twenties the bonanza was already over: less fish were being caught and their average size was diminishing. The second world war earned another respite for the fish of the North Sea, who responded once again by increasing their stocks and their average size.

The lessons of the North Sea led scientists to study the effects of fishing on fish populations. That study continues today and is far from complete. Some of the early discoveries and concepts are still of interest and practical value. It was found, for instance, that the catching of old fish might be beneficial to the fishery as a whole as older fish may often succeed in obtaining food at the expense of younger fish which may in turn be starved out and die. The removal of the older fish permits more of the younger fish to mature to adulthood (it is young adult fish, rather than immature and old fish, that tend to be of interest to retailers of fish). The useful concept of a sustained yield was also applied to fishing. Put simply, this is the maximum yield which can be removed each season without taxing the reproductive capacities of a fishery to such an extent that those fish removed are not entirely replaced—in other words, it is the maximum you can take in one season without taking the risk of reducing the numbers that will be around when you come back in future seasons. Sustained yields make obvious economic sense, yet the fishing industry has shown itself to be as incapable of sticking to them as the whaling industry.

Since the second world war big business and high technology have bestowed their dubious blessings on the fishing industry and have seemingly served merely to accelerate its passage along the dismal trajectory of discovery, bonanza, overkill and collapse. Their much vaunted increases in yield have been so "successful" that fishery after fishery has sunk into commercial extinction. So far there has always been another fishery over the horizon, but those days could be coming to an end: there are not too many fisheries left. S. J. Holt, a senior official in the FAO, predicts that "the maximum sustainable world catch of between 100 and 200 million tons could be reached by . . . 1985, or at least by the end of the century." Unfortunately, if this prediction is fulfilled it will probaly be due to nonsensical means which will also ensure that the maximum sustainable yield is rapidly exceeded. Existing practices in the fishing industry could rob this planet of one of its most important assets, its last reservoir of "wild" protein. Fish farm themselves, if allowed to do so.

The world fish catch increased tenfold in the century from 1850 to 1950, doubled in the next decade and increased by a half in the decade after that. The 1970 catch of 69.3 million

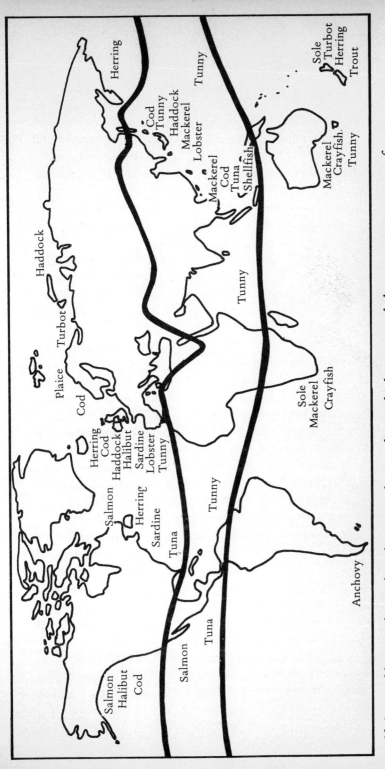

Half the world's population lives between the two lines which run round the equator yet many of the world's principal fishing grounds can be seen to lie in more temperate regions outside the lines.

tons might not seem too large compared to the projected maximum sustainable world catch of "between 100 and 200 million tons." It is only when one examines the narrow base of this catch that doubts creep in and the disastrous 1969 catch, the first decline since the war, becomes understandable. Rather than spread the load among a variety of species of fish of varying size in a wide range of locations, the fishing industry has concentrated its attack. It makes economic sense to concentrate on those particular species which sell best and to attack them when and where they themselves concentrate—for example, when they gather to breed or when they shoal to migrate.

Almost a third of the current world catch consists of five species alone, out of 20,000 species of marine fish. Top of the list is the Peruvian anchoveta, weighing in at 10.4 million tons (according to the FAO's 1967 statistics). It is followed by the Atlantic herring (3.8 million tons). Both these species are raw material for the fishmeal and fish oil industries and have the obliging habit of forming enormous shoals. The other three of the big five, the Atlantic cod, the Alaska walleye pollack and the South African pilchard (another meal and oil fish) weigh in at 3.1, 1.7 and 1.1 million tons respectively. These fish come from a small area, and it is claimed that an area approximately as large as California produces about half the world's fish supply. The claim is based not on the full range of all the fish, but on the area they occupy at any one time, but even when the full range is taken into account, 60 percent of the world catch is found to come from three limited areas. These are the North East Atlantic, the West Central Pacific and the upwelling off the coast of Peru.

This concentration is only partially explained by the naturally limited distribution of fish. There are still fisheries that are completely untapped while others have been fished to exhaustion. Once again commercial criteria have played an important role. The fishmeal industry, which is the single largest market for landed fish, requires large expensive plants. The processing plants need to be sited as close as possible to the fisheries which supply them and, once built, they need to be continually supplied with fish. If the supply exceeds the sustainable yield of the fishery, as it usually does after a very short time, that's too bad. The Peruvian anchovy industry is an edifying example. In just one decade this grew from a minor fishery with a catch of well under half a million tons to the world's biggest single-species fishery, with annual catches over 10 million tons, making Peru the world's leading fishing nation. Although the fishery had been fished on a very small scale since the thirties, it did not turn into a bonanza till a lot of capital had been invested in processing factories onshore. The catch increased fourteenfold in just five years (1957–1962). In the next five years it only increased by a half and in two of those years, 1963 and 1965, it actually declined. In 1968 the catch rose to 10.6 million tons and promptly slumped again in 1969 to 9.2 million tons. In 1970 gargantuan efforts caused a vast catch of 12.6 million tons to be landed. This was probably well above the sustainable yield. In 1971 the Peruvian government finally called a halt and actually banned fishing for three months and imposed further restrictions to limit the season's catch to 10 million tons. This figure probably also exceeds the sustainable yield and was not, alas, arrived at on grounds of resource conservation but on straightforward commercial grounds. A 10 million-ton catch of anchovies could produce enough protein concentrate to offset the protein deficiencies of most of the inhabitants of Latin America. Instead it is reduced to 2 million tons of fishmeal and exported for much needed cash. This concentration on one species in one confined area has had its impact heightened by a blind disregard for the size of fish caught. Any fish will do for a meal factory, so minute fish, too small to eat, are included in the catch. The results of the removal of these young fish should be felt soon. (The Peruvian government did decide to restrict fishmeal production in 1971, but that was merely to keep prices high.)

The modern fishing industry would not have been able to grow at such a spectacular rate and to concentrate its efforts in such financially rewarding ways if it were not for the attentions of technology. New methods of fish spotting, catching, preservation and processing continually increase the proportion of fish that man is able to remove from any given fishery and push the point of commercial extinction further beyond the sustainable yield. Shoals can be spotted from the air and from boats equipped with electronic sensors. Nets are decreasing in mesh size but becoming much larger in overall size. The handling of nets is being automated so that it becomes a faster, safer activity. Boats are getting bigger, can travel farther and pinpoint their position and hold their course more accurately—thanks to radar and other navigational equipment. The Russians and Japanese are building large numbers of factory ships which can freeze fish or turn them into meal at sea and raise the fishing time available to the fishing boats serving them.

The large amounts of capital necessary to finance this escalating technocratic assault on the fishery resources of this planet make the process a self-fueling one. The equipment has to be used to maximum capacity to justify its expense. Once one section of the industry increases its armory others have to follow suit—since prices are determined by the overall size of the catch, everyone tries to land as big a slice as possible. These tendencies can only promote further disregard for sustained yields and widen the gap between the rich and poor nations. As overexploited fisheries collapse in the traditional areas, hyperefficient fleets from developed countries will be commercially impelled to encroach on fisheries in more distant underdeveloped areas. Underdeveloped countries, by definition, are unable to compete with capital-intensive technologies so the result can only be sad for them. In addition, economic pressures will cause more and more of their catch to be processed and exported away from starving stomachs towards the broiler chicken factories of the developed nations.

The rapidity with which this game of grabs is heading for its natural limits can be grasped by taking a tally of the fisheries which have already been exhausted, those that are in the process of exhaustion and those left for future exhaustion. In 1949 the United Nations held a scientific conference on the conservation and utilization of resources. Its conclusion was that the only overexploited stocks were of a few high-priced species, such as plaice, halibut and salmon, in the North Atlantic and North Pacific. It was further concluded that thirty other known major stocks were underexploited. When the situation was reassessed just twenty years later it was found half of them were now over-exploited or on the verge of overexploitation. In the North Atlantic alone eight major fisheries were found to be in this state. Cod and tuna are beating a fast retreat all over the planet. There are surprisingly few virgin fisheries left, most of them in the southern hemisphere where the record of the rapid exploitation of the Peruvian anchovy can hardly be regarded as a good omen.

The fact that overexploitation makes economic nonsense in anything but the shortest of short-term views has filtered through to the industry, but the controls that have resulted have been few and far between and the overall picture is one of inadequacy. There are various ways in which the plunder is curbed, willingly or unwillingly. The most effective are regional treaties, in particular those regulating fisheries where only a few nations are involved. The East Pacific halibut fishery, for example, is only fished by the United States and Canada. Consequently, when catches slumped to 44 million pounds in 1931 (after a high of 69 million pounds in 1915) it was relatively easy for conservation measures to be taken. The two nations agreed to establish a commission to regulate the fishery. The commissions established size limits for the total annual catch and for individual fish sizes (to reduce the number of immature fish removed). As a result stocks are thought to have trebled. The International Pacific Halibut Commission is very much the exception. Other regional intergovernmental organizations have been less successful—because their jobs have been far more complex. These organizations include: Indo-Pacific Fisheries Council (16 nations), Inter-American Tropical Tuna Commission (3 nations), International Commission for Northwest Atlantic Fisheries (10 nations), International Council for the Exploration of the Sea (13 nations), International North Pacific Fisheries Commission (3 nations), International Pacific Salmon Fisheries Commission (2 nations), International Whaling Commission (17 nations), Atlantic States Marine Fisheries Commission (5 states), and Pacific States Marine Fisheries Commission (3 states). The International Council for the Exploration of the Sea, which has been tackling these complex problems for longer than the others, is more successful than most as it has managed to build up cooperation between east and west European nations. It has not yet developed as a strong regulatory body but has at least taken the essential first steps in that direction by initiating constructive dialogue between countries which would otherwise conflict over their fishing interests.

The problems facing the regulatory organizations are well summed up in the 1967 Report of America's National Academy of Science Committee on Oceanography (NASCO):

> Ocean fishing power on a world-wide basis is growing at a much more rapid rate than the means of measuring its effect on the fish stocks it is being applied against . . . This whole field of marine science is being swamped by the developing fishing power. The nations devote their ocean research funds to the development of fisheries, but they are laggardly in providing research funds for the detailed biological and population dynamics research which alone can give guidance in the solution of the problems which expanded fishing creates.
> Nations do not like to put their fishermen under regulation even to provide the conservation that they have agreed to provide unless the scientific needs for the regulation are established and they do not like to put up money to provide the research needed either to determine the need for regulation or the form it should take.

There has yet to be a single scientifically managed fishery in the seas. Regulation does not occur until disaster has occurred or is imminent and then it merely acts as a haphazard and ineffective brake, instead of a positive mechanism to bring about a maximum sustainable yield.

The FAO's Department of Fisheries is the only global organization concerned with the regulation of fisheries. Up till now it has been underfinanced and unable to do a great deal more than coordinate the research of other organizations and help the establishment of regional regulatory organizations in the Indo-Pacific area, the Mediterranean Sea, the East-central Atlantic, the Southwestern Atlantic and the Southeastern Atlantic. The Department needs, but is unlikely to receive, much greater resources so that it can establish international standards for regulating fisheries and so that it could help apply such standards. Whereas the national factions of the whaling industry have managed to establish quotas limiting the total annual catch of each nation, the fishing industry has had no such success, This is a minimal requirement for any sanely managed fishery: further requirements may prove even more elusive.

The regulation of fisheries is complicated by the struggle over fishing limits that has been developing since the war. This is a somewhat desperate last resort of nations faced with an insane situation and able only to think of insane solutions. It makes a small amount of sense where a species of fish spends its entire life within the coastal region of one nation. Even so it is debatable whether one should allow only that nation to reap the benefits of such a rare accident. All that can be said in its favor is that it gives the government concerned the opportunity to instigate thorough scientifically based management programs. It is an opportunity rarely seized. A government sufficiently influenced by its fishing industry to risk international displeasure at its creation of fishing limits is unlikely to turn round and tell that industry how to run itself. Once again the poachers are left to do the gamekeeping. Most fish are highly mobile, so the advent of fishing limits has only meant that during their lifetime they are chased by fishermen of different nationalities. It is only when fishing limits are violated that effective action is taken to actually stop fishing. Japanese and Russian boats have been fined very large sums for violating American limits. It is a shame that such spurious legalities are not more rationally based.

Another form of national action was pioneered in America in December 1971 when President Nixon signed a bill giving himself the power, should he wish to exercise it, to impose restrictions on fish imports from nations harming international fishery conservation programs. This unusual display of morality is probably more of a trade protectionist stunt than a serious fish protectionist measure but it might in more responsible hands be a useful weapon for the future.

Most national actions with the alleged purpose of conserving fisheries make little sense, and can only be negative, in a global situation which amounts to chaos. Immediate international cooperation is needed to determine the sustained yields for all fisheries. The yields should be expressed in terms of the age of the fish as well as species and should be flexible enough to respond to naturally induced population changes within a fishery. The yields should be subdivided into national quotas based on a modicum of morality. There should also be quotas stipulating upper limits for different uses of the catch—such as the manufacture of fishmeal. The latter is highly unlikely to happen (for one thing, where else would developing countries get the revenue they receive at present from the export of fishmeal?). The other measures stand little chance of happening either. Small steps are, thank God, being taken but time is running out very fast. The Soviet Union announced in the summer of 1971 in its new five-year plan that it envisages a minimum increase of 47 percent in the production of edible fish. Most of this expansion is expected to result from the application of modern methods to fisheries in the Indian and Pacific Oceans. No mention of conservation of stocks is made in the entire plan. Other countries have similar plans.

Whales and fish are not the only victims of overkill. Crustacea, especially shrimps, are being widely overfished and have no organizations at all protecting them. In 1936 the U.S. shrimp industry was to boast an annual catch of 6.3 million pounds.

Two decades later the catch had crashed to 10,000 pounds. Pollution undoubtedly added to the effects of overfishing but it is too late to determine which was the more important and how the two factors interacted.

It is also too late to determine the ecological impact of the shrimps' disappearance. There is no doubt that the mass removal of living organisms from the sea has a bad effect on those left behind, though usually we only discover undesirable effects when they have commercial implications. The Peruvian anchovy industry, once again, furnishes an example. Anchovy happen to form an important source of food for the guano bird—producer of the rich nitrogenous guano fertilizer. When man suddenly started to remove anchovy from the seas in large numbers the population of the bird crashed from 28 million to 4 million in one decade and is still declining. No doubt the widespread removal of small plant-eating fish is having an influence on populations of bigger fish that eat them. Even simple relationships such as this have yet to be examined in detail.

We shall see in subsequent chapters that the physical and chemical changes to the marine environment being brought about by the activities of man are also affecting marine mammals, fish and crustacea. Some are killed, others are diseased a decline in quality; very large numbers are now deemed unfit and deformed. The decline in quantity is being accompanied by for human consumption. The combined effect of pollution and overkill is to put at risk one of man's greatest natural food resources when he needs it most.

Overfertility

4

Man's first large-scale introduction of pollutants
into the marine environment came with the agricultural revolution and the establishment of permanent settlements. As the settlements grew in size,
less human and animal wastes were returned to
the soil. This broke the natural cycle which maintains the productivity of the soil. The organic
wastes of the animals, including man's, which feed
on plants represent material and energy resources
removed from the soil. If they are not returned to
the soil it gradually loses its fertility and those
structural properties, such as water retentiveness,
which make it an invaluable substratum for plant
growth. Instead of maintaining the fertility of the
soil upon which their wealth was dependent, the
early settlements started to pipe it off to the nearest body of water. While the quantities remained
low this wastage does not seem to have done any
notable damage to water life; it may even have
helped to increase the numbers of fish available
for food, as the fertility of the wastes would
nourish the water plants which are the basis of
fish life. It seems probable that most early civilizations felt the impact of soil infertility long
before their rivers and lakes displayed any of the

signs of ecological imbalance which can result from over-fertility.

The Minoan, Roman and Greek civilizations all experienced crippling famines when their soil failed them. The German chemist Liebig said of Rome: "The sewers of the immense metropolis engulfed in the course of centuries the prosperity of Roman peasants. The Roman Campagna could no longer yield the means of feeding her population; these same sewers de-voured the wealth of Sicily, Sardinia and the fertile lands of the coast of Africa." The Maya civilization of Central America brought itself to the point of collapse long before the Spaniards colonized their lands because of unsound methods of waste dis-posal. Their beautiful cities were surrounded by agricultural land which was rapidly robbed of its fertility as food was taken from it into the centers and wastes were never returned.

The Chinese civilization is one of the few based on the care-ful conservation of soil fertility: for 2,000 years they have re-turned their animal and vegetable wastes to their land. Few other societies have learned from the Chinese example. Indus-trial man has exacerbated the tendencies of earlier civilizations by concentrating in expanding cities and by increasing the amount of fertility he removes from the soil. Today the pres-sures on agricultural land are such that it is unthinkable to move on, as the Mayans did, once the natural fertility of the soil has been removed. Instead we take the extraordinary mea-sure of using enormous quantities of energy and material re-sources to replace lost fertility or to augment natural fertility and to increase yields. This makes current food production methods, including those with comparatively high yields, very inefficient. Farmers become trapped in a financially hair-raising process of addiction. Their soil quickly becomes addicted to inorganic fertilizers: more and more has to be used to keep yields constant. The annual consumption of inorganic nitrogen fertilizers has increased fourteenfold in the United States in the past twenty-five years, while agricultural crop production has not even doubled during the same period. As much as half of the inorganic nitrogen fertilizer which is applied to the land never reaches the plants but is washed out into neighboring bodies of water. Inorganic phosphorus and potassium fertilizers, which are used in lesser quantities than nitrogen, are equally wastefully used. It is not surprising that analyses show that the nitrogen content of waterways in agricultural areas has shot up in the last two decades.

The world-wide process of urbanization has increased the quantities and concentrations of organic wastes introduced by man into waterways and, ultimately, into the world ocean into which they flow. Sophisticated sewage treatment plants may have added to, rather than subtracted from, the problem. In the United States 1,300 of the 7,500 communities with sewers still dump their sewage straight into a waterway without any prior treatment. In the U.K. sewage from about 6 million people is discharged to the sea or estuaries. All the other American communities have primary treatment plants which reduce the organic content of wastes by 35 percent by passing them through a settling tank. Five out of eight of the communities with primary treatment also have secondary treatment plants. These remove 80 to 90 percent of the organic matter in one of two ways. Both methods involve breaking down the organic wastes, using bacteria and other microorganisms, to a clear, dilute solution of inorganic chemicals. Inorganic nitrogen and phosphorus are the predominant elements present. Tertiary treatment, which removes the remaining 10 to 20 percent of organic wastes, is very rare in the United States and the rest of the world. However it is done is expensive and takes up a lot of land and is unlikely to become widespread.

The inorganic nitrogen and phosphorus present after primary and secondary treatment consists not only of the breakdown products of the decomposition of organic wastes but also of inorganic domestic wastes present in the sewage from the start. The most significant source of domestic inorganic material is synthetic detergents—which are usually rich in phosphate. Like inorganic fertilizers and secondary sewage treatment plants, synthetic detergents have burgeoned with the postwar industrial and technological boom. In the United Kingdom about 21 percent of the phosphorus in sewage is contributed by synthetic detergents. In the United States the proportion is not known but is probably much higher. Total phosphate discharge into waterways is thought to have increased by a factor of three or four in the last fifty years. Of this, 72 percent is thought to have resulted from discharges into sewers and a large proportion of that is derived from phosphate detergents. Recent alarm about the use of phosphate detergents has caused a switch, still very insignificant in terms of global usage, to other synthetic detergents. These are mostly nitrogen based and, as we shall see, equally dubious because of ecological effects when discharged into water.

As well as increasing the amount of inorganic fertilizing elements, such as nitrogen and phosphorus, that he introduces into the aquatic environment, industrial man has vastly increased his output of organic wastes. These wastes are produced by the industrial processes associated with slaughterhouses, laundries, breweries, dairies, sugar factories and other food processing plants.

The effect of all these wastes on the aquatic environments into which they are discharged is no longer insignificant. The much increased quantities of organic wastes and inorganic fertilizing elements produced by sewage treatment impose strong loads on water life. Both fresh water and sea water ecosystems cope naturally with organic wastes by decomposing them and breaking them down into inorganic elements. Decomposition can only be achieved by the removal of oxygen from the water. In a balanced system the removal of oxygen is compensated by the oxygen produced by plants which in turn are fertilized by the products of the decomposition. The cycle is broken if large amounts of material ready for decomposition are introduced. Too much oxygen is removed for the animals which eat the plants to survive. Once fish and other organisms die off in large numbers they merely add to the wastes and to the decomposition taking place. The diversity of species, upon which the stability of ecosystems is dependent, is diminished and in the end nearly all life can be eliminated from an area where decomposition has been rife.

The potential impact of organic wastes on aquatic environments is expressed in terms of the amount of oxygen that will be removed for its decomposition—its biological oxygen demand (BOD). The inorganic elements discharged by sewage which has undergone secondary sewage treatment, and by that which has undergone primary treatment but contains synthetic detergents, can have a far greater impact than untreated organic wastes. They act as inorganic fertilizers and cause massive increases in the population and productivity of plant life. The explosion in plant population is quickly followed by a mass death of the same plants—as they rarely live longer than a few days. The BOD of such a large mass of dead plants can be five or six times as much as that of the sewage if it had been discharged untreated. The sudden surge in decomposition which follows overfertilization leads to ecological imbalance and instability similar to that when untreated wastes are present in large quantities. The complete process from overfertilization to excessive decomposition is known as eutrophication and was first observed in bodies of fresh water, such as lakes, which build up high concentrations of the fertilizing elements. In the fifties and sixties some of the more valuable fisheries of Lake Erie began to decline and scientists were amazed to discover that such a large body of water was possibly receiving so much organic and inorganic wastes that its dissolved oxygen content was falling. Since then eutrophication has been found to be widespread and Lake Erie is regarded as being in great danger of dying completely.

It came as even more of a shock to discover that the seas themselves are showing signs of deoxygenation, a reduction in the diversity of species, and eutrophication caused by waste disposal. The first signs came from enclosed, slightly stagnant lake-like bodies of sea water such as the Baltic, the fiords of Norway, and harbours.

The Baltic Sea is fifteen times the size of Lake Erie. It is the ultimate recipient of gargantuan discharges of all manner of wastes from the six heavily industrialized nations which border it. The fact that it receives a wide variety of toxins and that it is naturally stagnant (and therefore low in oxygen, especially in its deeper parts) makes it difficult for scientists to determine the full effects of organic oxygen-demanding wastes and of over-fertilizing inorganic elements such as nitrogen and phosphorus. This is partially mitigated by the fact that the Baltic is probably the most studied body of sea water in the world and by the initiation of a "Baltic Year" in 1969. Some of the fruits of this research will be included in a fuller description of the decline of the Baltic in a later chapter; at this point it is sufficient to note that it appears that the wastes previously mentioned are of critical importance as they accentuate the natural processes of stagnation. The entire deepwater area of the Baltic Sea is turning into a biological desert without any visible life—just the anaerobic bacteria responsible for decomposition.

Studies of the Oslofiord show that the discharge of sewage is the main cause of a steady decline in stocks of commercial animals. Like the neighboring Baltic, the Oslofiord is naturally slightly stagnant and is the recipient of many wastes with a high biological oxygen demand. Research has shown that these wastes cause most damage by deoxygenation of the water. Adult fish move away to more richly oxygenated waters, their eggs are unable to hatch and any larvae that drift into the area are unable to develop. Furthermore, the organisms upon which they feed are similarly affected and, therefore, are unavailable or only available in restricted quantity. Eggs and larvae are also adversely affected by the increased turbidity of the water and by the decomposing bacteria.

Large amounts of evidence are accumulating that less enclosed bodies of sea water are being similarly affected. The continental shelves of industrial countries are displaying the same symptoms of decay. The nursery grounds of many commercial species of fish are being eliminated, and highly productive ecosystems such as seaweed forests and estuaries are being relentlessly simplified and destroyed. The forests of the seaweed kelp that are found on the continental shelves of much of the temperate zone can support many species of fish, shellfish, starfish, sea urchins, worms and microorganisms. Now they are frequently inhabited by a skeleton crew of decomposer organisms —mainly worms and bacteria. Estuaries are the spawning grounds of many of the fish we eat and they form the base of the food chain of approximately 60 percent of the food we take from the sea. It is sad that big rivers have always acted as a focus for human settlement and that industrial society is no exception.

Overfertilization had led to an increase in coastal areas of the instance of so-called "red tides." The tides are caused by explosions in the population of certain red species of phytoplankton. They are highly unwelcome because they pose threats both to fishing stocks and to human health, and just because they are so unpleasant they have been precisely documented. Records show that a red tide occurred off the Florida Gulf Coast in 1916. The next one did not occur until 1932 and the one after until 1948. There were tides in 1952, 1953, 1954 and every year from 1957 to today. Other tides of differently colored phytoplankton occur off the coasts of Ceylon, Brazil and Spain. These tides may be sufficiently dense to clog the gills of fish and the filters of shellfish. Some produce poisons which kill or paralyze animals, including fish, at all stages of development. Shellfish which are not killed outright can still build up high concentrations of the poison and may kill a man who eats them. Sea spray containing tide phytoplankton can harm man on contact, causing irritations of the skin, mouth and throat.

Tides of toxic phytoplankton are not the only health hazards resulting from the discharge of sewage into the sea. The East coast of America, particularly that section of it which receives the wastes of the New York area, has been found to be rich in microorganisms considered dangerous to man. More than forty-five strains of virus—including those which cause polio and meningitis—have been found in water off the New Jersey coast. Government scientists found that the organic content of sewage acts as a protective coating, so that the viruses tend to live longer and are more likely to contaminate waters used for swimming, sailing and surfing. Until recently it was accepted that sea water effectively killed the bacteria associated with human wastes, but this belief was rudely shattered in a study conducted by the Adelphia University Institute of Marine Sciences. Bacteria were detected along the entire length of the Hudson Canyon, a deep marine canyon which extends from the mouth of New York's Hudson River to the edge of the continental shelf—a distance of about 110 miles. Raw sewage is dumped by the City of New York and other municipalities in the area above the Canyon thirty miles from shore. There is, in this vicinity, an area of "dead sea" which covered almost fifty square kilometers when last measured. The dead sea is almost devoid of animal life and has only the smallest populations of a few species of other forms of life. A large part of the area is covered by as much as five feet of rotting sediment which smothers any bottom-living forms of life. The scientists found 900 coliform bacteria per cubic centimeter of water in the dumping "dead sea" area. They found 46,000 per cubic centimeter at the start of the canyon but were far more disturbed to find 400 per centimeter in the canyon waters right at the edge of the continental shelf, eighty miles from the principal dumping area. This shattered the previous belief that in three miles of travel from the dumping area all coliform bacteria are killed. Coliform bacteria are not in themselves considered dangerous to human health but the number of them in any given volume of water is used as an indicator of the presence of other forms of bacteria and viruses that might be dangerous. Other forms of bacteria might be absorbed by shellfish and transmitted to man in this form or they could become attached to the skin of bathers. Some commercial shellfisheries along the Hudson Canyon will probably have to be closed down as a result of the discovery. The investigation of other areas of continental shelf near industrial areas would probably indicate other equally disturbing situations and lead to the closure of many shellfisheries.

It now seems that the east coast of the United States, the Baltic Sea, the North Sea, the Irish Sea and parts of the Mediterranean Sea are fast approaching the point where it will be unsafe to discharge effluent anywhere in them. At the same time increasing pressure on land for the conservation of fresh water for drinking will make it more and more tempting for local authorities to discharge their wastes into the sea. At present there is little national or local control of discharge into the sea. A minimum requirement ought to be that discharge areas should be carefully sited to avoid contamination of estuaries, salt marshes, fish breeding grounds, beds of shellfish and recreational areas such as bathing beaches. Some scientists go so far as to say no effluent at all should be discharged into waters above the continental shelves adjacent to heavily populated and industrialized regions. Local authorities would either have to ship their wastes at great expense to the open ocean or else find some way of disposing of them on land.

One or two enlightened localities have come to realize that wastes are indeed wastes if they are not restored to the soil and hence to the natural cycle to which they belong. It has also been suggested that the fertility of organic wastes could be put to beneficial use in the seas if carefully controlled, the most commonly mooted idea being that the diluted sewage might be fed into a series of ponds of sea water where it could stimulate phytoplankton growth and support large numbers of fish. Economic considerations make this less feasible than the ecologically more sound practice of returning the wastes to the soil. Wastes are indeed wasted when they are put where they do not belong.

The return would be cheapest to effect in developing countries where domestic wastes are not mixed with synthetic detergents and other household items. The current Chinese methods might act as a useful model. Most pig, sheep and human excrement is returned to fertilize the soil. It is collected every morning in the towns by trucks with pumps, by horse-drawn carts with tanks on the back and by bicycle-drawn tanks. The material collected in this way is taken to the rural communes where it is mixed with straw and animal manure and left in concrete covered pits for a fortnight. There are three different pits and the mixture is moved from one to the other until the heat produced by the composting has killed all germs and the manure is ready for use on the fields.

In industrial nations it is possible to treat all human wastes and industrial organic wastes in this fashion. Human wastes could only be treated if toilets were redesigned, and this is unlikely to happen until water shortages are sufficient to make the flushing of gallons of water an unreasonable act. There is already a Swedish unit for sale which converts all human wastes and organic kitchen wastes into a compost rich in fertilizers. It requires no electricity or water and is well enough designed to appeal to the most affluent consumer. Its sale is at present restricted to the owners of isolated houses which cannot be connected to sewage pipes or running water but is potentially much wider.

Meantime the industrial countries should apply research to devising cheap ways of removing the fertilizing elements from the complex mixtures that enter our sewage plants. Farmers and gardeners in England and other European countries are already able to buy treated sludge from some local authorities. It would be advisable for national governments to finance research into these fields and to encourage local authorities to apply what knowledge is already available. Failure to do so is both a waste of fertility and a threat to food supplies, health and recreational amenities.

Chlorinated Hydrocarbons

5

Traditional attacks on environmental pollution pay far more attention to seeming poisons than to "natural" wastes such as sewage. The first targets were pesticides such as DDT. Subsequent research, which would never have occurred if it were not for the dust raised by early environmentalists, showed that most of the damage attributed to DDT is in fact caused by one of its breakdown products, DDE, and by polychlorinated biphenyls (PCBs)—a group of chemicals with structures very similar to those of DDT compounds. Neither DDE nor the PCBs are themselves pesticides: it is more accurate to refer to them, and to the residues of other pesticides such as dieldrin, aldrin and azodrin, as chlorinated hydrocarbons. Although DDT and other biocides may not be significant environmental toxins, some of their breakdown products are, so they remain valid focuses for critical concern.

The United States chemical industry manufactures over 1 billion pounds of biocides every year. Its output consists of hundreds of different varieties which cost millions of dollars to develop, but these development costs are almost entirely spent ensuring that the agents perform their specific killing tasks effectively and economically. Little or no money is spent checking out the environmental impact of the substances once they leave the factory. It is left to scientists financed by the taxpayer to carry out such research. Consequently it is rarely done, and even when it is done it is done by definition too late: the substances are already in the environment. Once research is underway and evidence begins to accumulate that a particular substance is dangerous when released into the environment, the story is by no means over. It has just started. The media seize on the research and, thanks to self-imposed constraints, disseminate information about it in an inaccurate and alarming fashion. Headlines play on deep-seated fears of poisoning and food contamination. Sometimes they are right. Sometimes they are not. There are now so many potential toxins in the environment, many of which interact in complex ways, that it is inordinately difficult to unravel the passage of a single one and to state confidently that it alone is responsible for lethal or sublethal effects on particular living organisms.

Once the media have done their job ("Plastic Flowers Linked to Skin Cancer Says Leading Medic") all regard for complexity is thrown out the window. A ritual charade begins to unfold: on the one hand, a lobby emerges to control the offending substance; on the other, a faithful band of tame scientists is wheeled out by the manufacturer to ridicule the lobby in a "respectable" fashion and to assure the public that its product is utterly unimpeachable. As the scientific evidence accumulates and starts to speak louder than the earlier assertions of its publicists, and of its industrial counterpublicists, official bodies start to consider action. It often happens that the official advisory bodies are largely comprised of scientists from the companies manufacturing the offending substance. When action finally comes it is usually long overdue and inadequate. By that time an enormous quantity of the substance is at large and may persist in the environment for years—in some instances centuries.

The manufacturer stands to lose the money he used to develop the product. He often solves that problem in the short term by exporting it to people in such dire need that they cannot afford to be fussy, until even that avenue is eventually closed. If the manufacturer has problems, his customer has even greater ones. Just as the farmer finds that his soil becomes addicted to artificial fertilizers, so the biocide user finds himself an addict—suddenly deprived of his dope. The sustained use of biocides nearly always causes the "pest" involved to develop into resistant forms. Bigger and bigger doses have to be applied to keep it down. At the same time those creatures which would naturally keep the pest down are often reduced in number or completely wiped out. Removal of the biocide leaves the customer with a lot of tough pests and a low stock of natural control organisms.

The story of the chlorinated hydrocarbons embodies most of the elements of this tragicomedy. The granddaddy of them all, DDT, is a particularly edifying case. The first DDT (dichloro-diphenyl-trichloro-ethane) compound was synthesized in 1874 by a German chemist, but its insecticidal properties were not discovered until 1939. They were so phenomenal that their discoverer was promptly awarded a Nobel Prize and DDT compounds quickly entered the chemical arsenal of the farmer, though it was not until the postwar period that production really skyrocketed. Many different organizations started manufacturing DDT compounds, and this makes it difficult to arrive at national, let alone global, production figures. The *Chemical Economics Handbook* estimates that the total United States production rose from 4,400 metric tons in 1944 to a peak of 81,300 metric tons in 1963. It further estimates that a total of 1,220,000 metric tons of DDT compounds was manufactured in the United States alone in the period from 1944 to 1968.

What happened to this and to all the other DDT compounds manufactured in other countries? The vast majority of it was used by farmers to control insects, and the most common method of application is spraying—from the ground or the air. Right away losses occur as a fraction of the spray droplets is wafted away by winds and is carried off to be deposited elsewhere. A minute fraction of that which lands actually ends up in pests. Some of it is absorbed by the soil and stays there until it is broken down or is absorbed by soil organisms. Scientists disagree as to what proportion ends up in the soil, how long it takes to be broken down and what breakdown products are formed. They generally agree that it is to all intents and purposes nonbiodegradable—that is, it cannot be broken down into harmless elements by living things—and it therefore stays around for a long time (estimates vary from five to fifty years). One of the major breakdown products is now known to be DDE. The amount of the spray which lands on the soil surface and on plant surfaces is liable to evaporate and to enter the atmosphere which carries it away from the area. Further departures are caused by runoff into neighboring bodies of water.

As DDT compounds take a long time to break down, as a lot of them enter the atmosphere and surface water systems, as 70 percent of precipitation occurs over the world ocean and as nearly all surface waters drain into the world ocean, it would seem likely that the ocean has received a large quantity of the substances. Recent calculations indicate that as much as a quarter of the annual production of DDT compounds is transported to the world ocean. Early workers assumed that most of this came by rivers but measurements of the contents of river water and rain water have upset this assumption completely. Extrapolations from such measurement suggest that only one thousandth of the DDT residues in the ocean are brought there by runoff from land and that the overwhelming majority comes down in precipitation. An important implication of this discovery is that DDT residues are not restricted to shallow coastal waters but are also to be found universally distributed in the surface layer of the world ocean. Even the polar seas have been found to have their fair share.

The next question to be answered is: do marine organisms absorb DDT and, if so, what effect does it have on them? The first hint that DDT residues are indeed absorbed by marine organisms was their discovery in the body tissues of oceanic birds that rarely approach land, except to breed, and that feed exclusively on surface marine plankton. This discovery was made all the more alarming as the quantities involved exceeded those found in land birds. Subsequently fish-eating marine birds (such as pelicans and cormorants) were also found to be heavily contaminated. Since then residues have been found all over the globe in every kind of creature investigated. Antarctic penguins, Arctic krill, Atlantic phytoplankton, Californian shrimps and North Sea cod have all revealed stores of DDT residues. Commercial "DDT" is nearly always a mixture comprising 80 percent DDE compounds and 20 percent others including DDT itself. Much of the DDT element is broken down to DDE so the bulk of the "DDT" in the environment and in living things is in fact DDE. DDE takes longer than DDT to break down (possibly decades) and is not known to be broken down by any marine organism—a bacterium found in cheese is the only creature thought to be able to cope in any way with DDE.

DDE enters plankton directly through their porous cell walls and tends to be stored in their fatty parts, as DDT compounds are all far more easily dissolved in fats than in water. Once stored, the compounds are slow to leave and the organism gradually builds up a concentration hundreds of thousands of times greater than that in the surrounding sea water. Concentrations increase as one looks at organisms further and further up the food chain. This was first discovered on land, in fresh-water food chains leading up from plankton to small fish, bigger fish and finally birds. The concentration occurring as the DDE passed up this chain was so great that the predatory birds which ate the fish-eating birds were carrying around massive doses of it. Investigation of marine food chains showed that their greater lengths lead to even greater concentrations in those birds, mammals and fish at the end of the food chains. (The picture has been complicated somewhat by measurements made in the Atlantic in 1971 by scientists from the Woods Hole Oceanographic Institute, Massachusetts. They found plankton with concentrations as great as those in organisms further up the food chain.

This has led to a less rigid approach to the concentrative powers of marine food chains but is still too little understood for an alternative theory to be developed.)

There is a great deal of dispute as to the effects of DDE compounds once they have been absorbed by living organisms, but laboratory tests have shown that cultures of marine animals and plants in flowing sea water contaminated with DDE and DDT compounds (in concentrations already found in coastal waters) are adversely affected in growth, reproduction and mortality. These findings have been corroborated by many disturbing observations made in the field.

The greatest controversy has centered around the contention that DDE inhibits the vital process of photosynthesis in phytoplankton. This process is one of the most important to marine life: anything which threatens it puts all other marine life in jeopardy. Early reports that DDE inhibits marine photosynthesis were confirmed in a series of experiments conducted in America, and the results were published in 1968 in an article in the magazine *Science* which caused quite a stir. It was felt at the time that concentrations in the ocean were possibly too low to have the same effect as the concentrations in the laboratory, but subsequent measurements of mid-oceanic concentrations have shaken this confidence somewhat. Plankton have been found to be very heavily contaminated and the population of plankton appears to be falling dangerously. So little is known of the natural fluctuations in the populations of marine phytoplankton and of the factors which control their productivity or of the effects of other environmental contaminants that it is very difficult to point with confidence to DDE compounds and to accuse them of inhibiting photosynthesis. But the evidence gets more and more convincing, and one can only pray that the scientific community will arrive at a firm conclusion before it is too late.

The zooplankton, or microscopic animals, of the sea are known to be highly sensitive to DDE compounds. Calanoid copepods, which are very important sources of food for many fish, have been shown to be extraordinarily sensitive to concentrations of DDE lower even than those found in rain water. Their eggs fail completely to develop into adults and the population plunges to zero. Crustacea, such as shrimps and crabs, have been found to be as sensitive to low concentrations as zooplankton. Shrimps continuously exposed to very low levels (similar to those found in Texas river waters which flow into nursery areas of commercially important shrimp) had a 100 percent mortality rate in less than twenty days. Increases in the amount of DDE compounds in coastal waters off California is thought to have been a major factor in the collapse of her shrimp fisheries and the slightly slower decline of the Dungeness crab. Filter-feeding molluscs, such as the oyster, are highly efficient at the extraction of DDE compounds from the sea water they filter but it does not seem to affect them as seriously, except by slowing down their growth.

Marine fish of all kinds in all parts of the world ocean have been found to be contaminated with DDE compounds. the effects upon them have yet to be adequately studied despite the suspicion that some coastal fisheries have declined into commercial extinction because of DDE. However, some fresh-water species have been studied in some detail and have been found to be highly sensitive to fairly low concentrations. One hundred percent failure in the development of young fresh-water trout has been recorded in instances where the fish concerned had lower internal concentrations of DDE compounds than those found in some marine species. Investigations of seatrout in the Laguna Madre in Texas have shown that their population has steadily declined as DDE concentration has risen. There now appear to be no juvenile fish at all. Anchovies and Jack mackerel off the California coast are also thought to have fallen towards commercial extinction as a result of organochlorine contamination. The fishing of mackerel was finally called to a halt when the level of DDT residues found in the fish reached a level officially considered dangerous to human health. High concentrations have also been found in marine mammals such as sealions and whales (the highest levels of DDT residues found in any organism were recorded in dead sealions washed up on Californian beaches).

Although reproductive failures of commercial stocks of fish, crustacea and molluscs represent the most important short-term problems of DDE for man, far more attention has been afforded to the effects on seabirds. As one marine biologists observed, "dead birds float—and they get washed up on beaches frequented by man." However, although sea birds exposed to high concentrations of DDE compounds have been studied for some time, for much of that time the analytical methods used could not differentiate exactly between the various forms of DDT, DDD, DDE and PCB compounds. Some effects ascribed in early work as the result of DDT residues may be partially or totally due to the presence of PCBs. Be that as it may, it seems clear that DDE compounds do their fair share of damage to sea birds. Because of their position at the end of food chains, marine birds build up a very high concentration of DDE compounds, and most of this is found in fatty tissues such as reproductive organs and nervous tissue. DDE seems to be strongly linked to the birds' success in hatching. When high concentrations are present, birds lay eggs with shells so thin that they break during incubation, The sex hormones are also affected, and this leads to infertility. The combination of these two defects can be disastrous. The brown pelicans and double-crested cormorants of Southern California are no longer able to reproduce and are rapidly becoming extinct in that area. Studies of the populations of British sea birds show that most are in serious decline and that many could soon become extinct.

Another hotly debated area is the effects of DDE compounds on man. The discovery that the milk in the breasts of American mothers contains such high concentrations of DDT residues that it exceeds the official limits for bottled milk highlighted the worsening situation in many industrialized countries. The agrochemical industry has met the occasionally hysterical reactions of the public with its own equally irrational counterhysteria.

Rachel Carson started the ball rolling when she wrote her

excellent book, *Silent Spring.* She painstakingly catalogued the evidence available at that time which implied that DDT compounds were dangerous environmental contaminants and a possible threat to human health. Large amounts of the compounds indubitably do accumulate in human tissues and it seem plausible that they might have similar effects on us to those induced in other vertebrates. Research linking DDE compounds to cancer is perhaps too tenuous for firm conclusions to be drawn but the possibilities of disruption of sex hormones, interference with the nervous system and changes in the functioning of the liver should be considered. The manufacturers have shown themselves extremely reluctant to discuss such possibilities. They claim that the evidence is not strong enough with a persistence that makes one wonder if the evidence could ever be strong enough to satisfy them. The Velsicol Chemical Company, a substantial manufacturer of chlorinated hydrocarbon pesticides, wrote a revealing letter to the publishers of *Silent Spring* in a vain attempt to prevent its publication. Part of that letter read as follows:

> Unfortunately, in addition to the sincere opinions by natural food faddists, Audubon groups and others, members of the chemical industry in this country and in Western Europe must deal with sinister influences, whose attacks on the chemical industry have a dual purpose:
> (1) to create the false impression that all business is grasping and immoral, and
> (2) to reduce the use of agricultural chemicals in this country and in the countries of Western Europe, so that our supply of food will be reduced to east-curtain parity. Many innocent groups are financed and led into attacks on the chemical industry by these sinister parties.

Irresponsibly crass statements of this nature were by no means infrequent at the time of publication of *Silent Spring* and are still being made by scientists employed by chemical companies. Manufacturers are so sensitive to the work of independent scientists who investigate the environmental impact of their products that they automatically treat them as antagonists, so that chances for the fruitful exchange of information and for intelligent scientific debate are minimized. The situation is made all the more reprehensible when one considers that the research conducted by publically funded independent scientists should have been done by the manufacturer before the product was indiscriminately released into the environment. As things stand an enormous amount of damage can be done before a substance is finally brought under control.

If the manufacture and use of DDT compounds were stopped tomorrow the quantity in the eivironment would be so large and its persistence in the environment so great that it could still be doing its damage in a decade from now. The damage to the oceans might well be greater in a few years time when residues held in lakes and other surface waters are finally released to sea water.

Public pressure and mounting scientific evidence have at last led to controls on the manufacture and use of DDT compounds which are long overdue. The delays caused by the reluctance of the powerful manufacturers to exercise control over their products in a responsible fashion were coupled to the inertia of users who had become addicted to DDT compounds and would be in a tight spot without them. It was argued that farmers could not do without the compounds and that the compounds should not, therefore, be banned. Hypocritical references were made to the plight of developing countries whose citizens might starve in a DDT-free agriculture. This approach ignores two important considerations.

First, as we have seen, DDT compounds are more than an environmental hazard; they are an economic trap. Spectacular short-term control of pests is bought at the cost of addiction and ultimate failure; more and more pesticide has to be bought to keep pests down in a given area until they develop resistance and the farmer is left with no natural or chemical controls which can be relied upon to cope with the superbugs. Second, the choice is not between indiscriminate use of DDT compounds and indiscriminate banning of them. Some uses of DDT compounds are so critically important that they cannot be stopped overnight. Their use for the control of malarial mosquitoes is one example. Many species are developing resistance to most DDT compounds but those that remain amenable should be sprayed until an alternative control is found. (Research is going on in Gambia and other malarial countries to find a vaccine to protect populations against the disease, and such research should receive greater funding than at present.)

However, most DDT compounds are used to control agricultural pests and it is this use which could be phased out fairly rapidly. Most current controls are hectic overnight affairs which offer no alternative to the farmer than to turn to the indiscriminate use of another pesticide (often another chlorinated hydrocarbon such as dieldrin and aldrin). The slightly hysterical nature of the debate which leads to the banning of a pesticide precludes rational discussion of strategies for its replacement. It is this lack which causes considerable concern to those who are dependent on pesticides.

The Food and Agriculture Organization (FAO) of the United Nations has experienced unnecessary division and misunderstanding because of this. The dispute came to a peak at the sixteenth Governing Conference of the FAO held in November 1971. Dr. Norman E. Borlaug, recipient of the 1970 Nobel Peace Prize, denounced "hysterical environmentalists" for their attempts to block the use of pesticides such as DDT. He claimed that "no chemical has done as much as DDT to improve the health, economic and social benefits of the people of the developing nations" and rightly pointed out that the immediate adverse consequences of a ban on DDT would be felt much more by low income groups than by "privileged environmentalists." Dr. Borlaug's claims were answered by Dr. Sicco L. Mansholt, one of Europe's leading statesmen and vice-president of the European Commission. He started by saying, "I am one of the hysterical environmentalists Dr. Borlag talked about," and went on to say that "We can produce as much food in the U.S. and

Europe without DDT and pesticides." He told the conference that the world cannot continue to tolerate DDT use which he estimated to be progressing at a rate which puts a kilogram per person per decade into the land, sea and air.

Although Dr. Mansholt failed to say so, the methods which could be used in Europe and the United States to reduce DDT use to zero while maintaining productivity could also be applied to developing countries. It would just be a bit more difficult technically and a lot more difficult economically. The process would have to be far more subtle than an overnight ban, and puritanical banishment of all users is doomed to failure in the immediate future.

There are one or two users who cannot afford to stop using DDT compounds and no one seems overanxious to help them. If, for example, malarial mosquitoes were to be kept down by malathion or propoxur (which are less persistent in the environment and less toxic to humans) the cost, which is born almost entirely by developing countries, would be trebled at the least and might be as much as eight times greater. As an immediate step it could be more feasable to devise and apply ways of diminishing the losses during spraying which represent a considerable waste of money and human effort.

Other uses of DDT compounds present less intractable problems, since far less persistent pesticides exist (organophosphates and carbamates, for example) and could be put to use right away. The long-term aim should, however, be to minimize the use of pesticides and to develop natural controls. Integrated control is a concept receiving a good deal of attention in the agricultural press of countries disenchanted with the crudities of "napalm farming" (the chemical control of pests). Its aim is the control of pests by a combination of biological control, mechanical control, the diversification of crop species and the highly discriminate use of non-persistent pesticides that act only on specific species. Biological control can be achieved by the encouragement or introduction of natural predators, natural insect repellents (such as garlic compounds), natural attractants and sterilizing compounds. Mechanical control is achieved by disrupting the habitats of pests or by mechanically removing pests from their habitat. Increased diversity of crop species establishes a more complex ecosystem than extensive monoculture and is more conducive to the establishment of natural predators. Species which resist the depredations of local pests can also be developed. Relatively safe, precise pesticides already exist but more could be developed.

The subtle integration of these controls would be as much an educational problem as an economic one. Current farming practices seem simplistic when compared to those that will be required. In some areas traditional biological and mechanical controls and local species of crop are well suited to the task, but these areas are small compared to the total task and nothing short of an international program will be successful. Developing countries will need both financial and educational assistance: developed countries will require educational assistance and the legislative power to redirect the energies of pesticide manufacturers to more responsible ends.

Current trends in pesticide control do not bode well for the future. Governments are slow to act (often because their pesticide control agencies are manned by personnel from pesticide manufacturers) and can only act in a negative fashion which puts the manufacturers in an uncooperative mood and offers no constructive alternative program of pest control. In 1970 and 1971 various national governments (including those of Denmark, Hungary, Sweden, the Soviet Union and the United States) imposed restrictions on the use of DDT compounds. Not one of those governments has an integrated policy for a switch to nonpersistent pesticides. Manufacturers are simply marketing their products elsewhere—to the developing countries in particular—and encouraging their customers at home to switch to other chlorinated hydrocarbon pesticides that have not been banned yet. World production of DDT is falling at last but there are few signs of a sane replacement. It is particularly sad that DDT is likely to be used for longer than necessary in the developing countries. It is argued that they can least afford a slackening of agriculture production, but it would be sad if such a limited view led to a contamination of the seas serious enough to affect stocks of fish protein.

In the last few years scientists have discovered that many of the substances they had been identifying as "DDT" were in fact polychlorinated biphenyls (PCBs). Their detection in all kinds of organisms all through the world ocean came as an immense surprise. None of the PCBs are pesticides and none of them are deliberately released into the environment. Somehow they are accidentally escaping and dispersing. The PCBs have a wide range of industrial applications, being used in the manfacture of paints, plastics, adhesives, coating compounds and electrical equipment. It is ironic that PCBs are occurring in increasing amounts in cardboard packaging made from recycled paper (it is thought that it enters this form via printing inks in which it is used as a solvent). It owes its industrial usefulness to its chemical stability, and this same property means that it persists in the environment for a long time after the disposal of the products of which it is a part. Marine food chains seem to concentrate it as effectively as they do the DDT compounds.

PCBs were only detected in the environment as recently as 1966. The Swedish scientist Soren Jensen discovered PCBs in pike and then looked elsewhere for further residues. He found appreciable amounts in the hair of his entire family—including a five-month-old baby. When he examined eagle feathers in a Swedish museum he discovered that the compounds were only present in specimens obtained after 1944 and deduced that PCBs had only been an environmental contaminant in the period after that date. Jensen's work was quickly followed by research in Britain, the Netherlands and North America which established that hitherto unidentifiable compounds which had been regularly discovered in association with DDT and DDE residues were PCBs. Having gone unnoticed for two decades, PCBs were suddenly discovered everywhere. Organisms from heavily industrialized areas of the northern hemisphere were found to have particularly high concentrations. Like DDT, it has even been found in the milk of Californian mothers.

American investigators have found a correlation between high levels of PCBs in adult sea lions and aborted foetuses. Over 1,000 aborted sea-lion pups were washed up on Californian beaches in 1970 and 1971. Unusually high levels of PCBs were also found in the corpses of over 12,000 sea birds washed up on the western coast of Britain in 1969. There is now good reason to believe that the compounds are involved, together with DDT compounds, in the thinning of shells of sea birds and this alone has lead British scientists to press for a ban on the further manufacture of them.

The most insidious discoveries of PCBs in marine organisms were made in the mid-Atlantic. A survey stretching across the entire ocean from the Arctic to the Antarctic and from the Americas to Europe and Africa showed that PCBs were present in practically all specimens collected and usually in higher concentrations than DDT residues. Plants and animals sampled included phytoplankton, zooplankton, sargassum weed, flying fish, dolphins, sharks and tiny fish that migrate daily from the surface to depths of as much as 3,000 feet. The biggest shock was the finding that plankton contained roughly ten times as much PCBs as other marine organisms. This contradicted the theory that compounds usually increase in concentration as one moves up the food chain. Scientists still do not understand what happens to all the PCB that enters the plankton but appears not to enter the organisms that eat them. It could be tsat plankton with the highest concentrations die or become unacceptable as food for other organisms. If this is the case the entire oceanic ecosystem may be very seriously threatened.

Scientists were so shocked by the Atlantic findings that research should at last be possible to determine what effects PCBs have on plankton and other mid-oceanic forms of life. The little research that has been done on the effects on the behavior and reproductive performance of coastal organisms has led to concern about the effects on humans of PCB residues. It is a problem that we will be able to study for a long time: PCBs are estimated to have a persistence 100 times greater than that of DDT residues (in other words they will be present in the environment for at least another 500 years). Many developed countries check their foodstuffs for the presence of PCBs and occasionally have to ban food they consider to be too contaminated. In just three months of 1971 the U.S. Food and Drug Administration destroyed 50,000 turkeys, 80,000 chickens and 60,000 eggs. It is known that all the chickens obtained their PCBs from the fishmeal which formed their staple diet.

The control of PCBs has been an even more haphazard affair than the control of DDT compounds. Because of the great variety of uses to which the compounds are put, no attempt has been made to suggest alternative substances to perform the same functions safely. It is still not known how the PCBs in the mid-ocean get there. Working backwards, scientists are becoming increasingly convinced that most of it reaches the seas via the atmosphere—but how does it get into the atmosphere? The most probable source is the burning of paints, varnishes and coatings containing PCBs. Monsanto Chemicals, the sole manufacturer in Great Britain and the United States, has taken the unique step of banning sales in those countries to people who put PCBs to uncontrollable uses (that is, those in which there is a danger that they might escape to the environment through burning or careless application). Even those customers who use the compounds for controllable uses—in sealed systems such as transformers— are urged by the company to exercise the utmost care. Monsanto has even developed a disposal service to collect customers' waste PCBs and destroy them by high pressure incineration. Monsanto also has an agreement with Bayer, the sole German manufacturer, not to sell PCBs for uncontrollable uses in West Germany. The two companies are believed to have a blacklist of companies which might put the chemicals to uncontrollable uses while professing otherwise. Both have also agreed that a disappointed customer from one country will not be served in the other.

This system of voluntary control appears to have worked better in Britain than in America where Monsanto was slower to act and less decisive once it did so. This could well be due to the massive birdkills in Britain which were wholly or partially attributable to PCBs. By taking the initiative Monsanto avoided a total ban and hung on to one section of a profitable market. While their overall action has been effective and commendable it must be pointed out that prior to its voluntary partial ban Monsanto had refused to cooperate with scientists in the United States who wanted to know total annual production figures and a list of all products containing PCBs. Both requests were unreasonably refused. It is to be hoped that Monsanto will prove more cooperative in the future and that other companies, such as those manufacturing other chlorinated hydrocarbons, learn a lesson from them.

Because of their persistence the combined effects of the hundreds of thousands of tons of chlorinated hydrocarbons already in the marine environment will be felt for years to come. Although world DDT consumption possibly fell by a half between 1964 and 1971 and PCB releases to the environment are probably beginning to fall, there is little room for complacency. If it took us twenty years to discover that PCBs were contaminating the entire world ocean what other compounds have we also missed? When both the supporters and antagonists of DDT compounds make their cases in a largely irrational manner what hope is there for the sane control of chlorinated hydrocarbon pesticides?

Heavy Metals and Other Industrial Wastes

6

Although they were the first to receive widespread attention, the chlorinated hydrocarbons are far from being the only contaminants industrial man has introduced to the marine environment. Most industrial wastes are simple inorganic compounds which are released to the world ocean indirectly—via the atmosphere and surface waters. Many of the inorganic elements man has put into the seas were already present there in considerable amounts, and although the concentrations of the elements in sea water may be low, the total quantities in the ocean are enormous. It might seem unlikely that man's industrial activities could affect the composition of sea water; yet this is happening.

The natural controls which have kept the composition of sea water constant for hundreds of millions of years have been upset by a sudden massive input of heavy metals such as lead. There is evidence that industrial lead has raised average lead concentrations in the oceanic waters of the northern hemisphere by a factor of two or three/This is a frightening achievement with unknown consequences. Total world production of lead totaled 3,500,000 metric tons in 1966 and the annual figure has risen since then. A significant percentage of this enters the seas to add to the 150,000 metric tons which is added every year by natural processes. Measurements show that the percentage which comes to the seas by way of atmospheric washout has been increasing in the last few years and that mid-oceanic concentrations are rising as a consequence.

Once lead has entered the ocean no one is too sure what happens to it—or to any other heavy metal. One scientist has summed up the situation as: "diffusion is confusion." Natural mixing processes diffuse the lead in ways which are poorly understood, but these processes are counteracted by marine organisms which have an uncanny and unfortunate knack for concentrating simple chemicals. It has been claimed that "for any given chemical element there will be found at least one planktonic species capable of spectacularly concentrating it." Once the plankton concentrate a substance, that concentration is passed right up the food chain. Lead is no exception: high concentrations have been found in many organisms in the coastal waters of industrialized regions, Filter-feeders (such as oysters) in estuaries build up some of the highest concentrations, as a lot of the riverborn lead falls to the bottom sediment when fresh water meets sea water.

Little data exists on the toxicity of heavy metals on fish. Those fish in waters with low oxygen content (caused by natural stagnation or the disposal of organic wastes) are particularly liable to build up high lead levels as they need to increase their rate of breathing and so increase the volume of water passing through their system. All heavy metals have been found, when present in high levels, to retard the growth and to increase the mortality of a wide range of marine animals—including shrimps and polychaete worms.

Compared to lead, mercury has been introduced by man into the marine environment in minute quantities. It is one of the most valuable heavy metals and few people throw it away if they can help it. Nonetheless as much as one-third of the annual global consumption of 10,000 tons does somehow find its way into the environment. Some of it escapes into river water in pulp-mill effluents and in mercury-based pesticides] Still more is released to the atmosphere when fossil fuels are burned (coal and oil contain small quantities of mercury, and power plants which burn them are now thought to be the largest source of mercury in the environment).

That which does reach the seas is concentrated even more effectively than other heavy metals: many organisms contain concentrations thousands of times higher than those of surrounding sea water. Mercury is highly toxic in very low concentrations and may be lethal to all forms of living matter. Incredibly low levels, well below those commonly accepted as safe for drinking water, have been found by Florida scientists to retard the growth of marine phytoplankton and to inhibit photosynthesis. By the time it reaches man the concentrations can be high enough to kill.

The worst instance of mercury poisoning was that at Minamata Bay in Japan. The disease first occurred in 1953 and by 1956 had built up to a crescendo. In that year it was identified as methyl mercury poisoning (methyl mercury is a compound formed when mercury comes in contact with organic wastes). The poison had severely affected the central nervous systems of the victims causing numbness of the limbs and lips, defective sight, ataxia (failure of muscular coordination) and slow, slurred speech. Of the 116 cases officially recognized, 43 died and most of the rest have yet to recover completely.

A clue to the source of the methyl mercury was given by the local cats which frequented the fish quay. Most of them had shown extreme signs of poisoning long before the humans and many had jumped into the sea where they drowned. Investigations showed that the bay's fish and shellfish, eaten by both the cats and their owners, were heavily contaminated with mercury. The search for the source of the mercury then began. It led to the Shin-Hihon Chisso Hiryo Company's chemical factory. The company displayed an intransigence not unakin to that of companies in other parts of the world faced with similar accusations. It refused to give information about its production processes and to submit waste water for analysis. It also denied all responsibility for the outbreak and the government took no action. Meanwhile the fishermen and their families received no relief or compensation. They stormed an annual general meeting of the Chisso Company and built up the sympathies of the Japanese people until finally twenty-eight families began court proceedings against the company. Scientists had determined the processes which were probably releasing the bulk of the mercury and the company eventually closed down the equipment involved (although it has of course never had the grace to admit any responsibility for the outbreak of poisoning). A similar episode occurred at the mouth of the Agamo river in 1965. After four years and three months in the courts some of the families involved secured very substantial damages from the chemical company responsible. The families of the Minamata victims have yet to complete their court battle.

Swedish scientists started the current concern about mercurial contamination of the environment when they discovered, in 1964, high levels of mercury in the corpses of fresh-water fish and birds. Marine fish (including mackerel, herring and cod) were also found to be heavily contaminated. Similar findings were made all over the world. A climax was reached in 1970 when many governments started to analyze food in the shops for traces of mercury. In the United States excessive amounts of methyl mercury were found in five tins of tuna fish— which led to 1 million tins of the product being withdrawn from sale. British government scientists also made investigations. They were quick to quote reassuring figures but slow to publish their less comforting findings. The most disturbing finding was that fish protein concentrates, which were mentioned earlier as a very promising source of protein for the third world, contain high levels of mercury. Concentrates of menhaden, alewife, Atlantic herring, Californian anchovy, Gulf menhaden and ocean pout were all found to contain levels of mercury exceeding the "practical residue limits" established by the FAO for marine products, and several exceeded the level which had caused the tuna fish ban in the United States.

The mercury in the marine environment seems to be more dangerous to man than to shellfish and fish (which build up high levels without suffering lethal effects) but it does affect other forms of marine life. As well as drastically threatening the well-being of plankton it has been shown to inhibit the development of the larvae of certain barnacles and sea urchins.

One reason why surprisingly low concentrations of mercury, and other environmental contaminants, can cause serious damage to marine organisms is a phenomenon known as synergism. Synergism occurs when two compounds act simultaneously to produce effects far greater than would be produced by either acting in isolation. It is not necessary for the two compounds to combine chemically or to come into contact in any way. For example, when laboratory animals containing low levels of mercury were exposed to a chemical known at NTA a tenfold increase in foetal abnormalities occurred. NTA is a nitrogen-based substance which was used by manufacturers to replace phosphates in synthetic detergents. It has since been banned in Sweden, the United States and other countries.

The most famous synergism involving mercury is the action of methyl mercury. A body of water containing mercuric wastes in the sediment on its bottom will not contain many contaminated organisms as the metal tends to stay put. If, however, organic pollutants enter the water, bacterial action will break them down to simpler organic chemical components including the methyl group. Methyl mercury is then formed. This is a substance which is highly soluble in water and which therefore moves with the currents and soon enters living things. When methyl mercury is not synergistically formed, mercury concentrations usually increase with depth. As most marine life inhabits the surface layers of the world ocean this might seem convenient. Unfortunately the richest areas of the sea for marine life are the upwellings which bring the higher concentrations to the surface (a mechanism which could well have contributed to the high mercury levels found in fish protein concentrate).

These are only two examples of synergisms known to take place, and just as there are probably many contaminants in the seas that we have yet to identify so there could be many un-identified dangerous synergisms.

Cadmium is the heavy metal which promises to be the big-gest threat of the future to marine life. It too first displayed its killing power in Japan where possibly as many as 500 people have died of *itai-itai*—cadmium poisoning. Most of the Japanese cadmium was traced from the bodies of the diseased back to zinc smelting works. Zinc smelting produces cadmium wastes which are discharged into rivers and then travel to rice paddies and are incorporated into the food of local people. Once inside the body, the cadmium builds up in the liver and kidneys. It also concentrates in the bones, replacing the chemically similar calcium, and when this happens the bones become so brittle that they can be broken by a cough. After an initial period of intransigence Japan's largest zinc producers reduced their out-put considerably. The president of one of the largest took the dramatic step of resigning because of the delayed guilt he sud-denly experienced.

Laboratory experiments with rats show that cadmium can cause high blood pressure. Humans dying of cardiovascular diseases have been found to have high concentrations of cad-mium in their kidneys, and areas with high death rates from cardiovascular diseases have been found to have high levels of cadmium in the air. In neither case has it been demonstrated that anything more than coincidence is (or is not) involved.

It is worrying that very little research has been done to determine the extent to which cadmium is present in the en-vironment or to investigate the effects that it has on marine or-ganisms. As *itai-itai* was traced back to water-borne cadmium, and as the other heavy metals are known to seriously affect sea life, it would be reasonable to expect that such research would have useful results. Investigations of the Bristol Channel led to the discovery that shellfish and other organisms there con-tained the highest levels of lead ever recorded in Britain: some had levels fifty times those found in contaminated Japanese rice, and the shellfish contained over 200 times the amount permitted by United States health regulations for food. The most ominous finding was that fish caught in the Bristol Channel had much higher levels of cadmium than expected. This bodes ill for fish and fisheaters alike. The Bristol cadmium probably comes from zinc smelting works similar to those in Japan. The biggest works, and the most likely major source, has completely ceased production.

Copper is a heavy metal which does not often occur in high concentrations in the sea but when it does it can have spectacular effects. The most dramatic case occurred in March 1965 off the Dutch coast. Industrial copper sulphate had been poured into the sea, increasing the natural concentration of copper in sea water over a hundred times. Instead of quickly dispersing, as the dumpers had hoped it would do, the copper-enriched water traveled in a coherent mass which wrought havoc as it moved along the coast. One hundred thousand dead fish were found on the beaches and many more were observed swimming around in the sea in an uncoordinated fashion. Whole mussel beds were wiped out and some species of plankton died in large numbers. In other parts of the world there have been reports of "green oysters" made unpalatable by the large amounts of copper they contain. Incidents such as these are at present local and do not yet represent a global contamination, just as other heavy metals such as zinc, nickel and silver can be found to be locally concentrated and even dangerous but have still to spread throughout the world to a worrying extent. However, any one of them could be involved in unknown synergisms, so we should not be too smug about their current distribution.

The heavy metals are of course little more than a fraction of the half-million substances released by industry into the environment. Few of them have such a marked effect as the heavy metals do on a global scale, but their local impacts are severe enough when combined with other forms of pollution to warrant concern. The practice of dumping industrial wastes from specially chartered ships into the ocean is growing, and it menaces life on the continental shelves and coastal areas of in-

dustrialized regions to a disturbing extent. Tighter controls on
land have made the seas an increasingly attractive dump to
producers of toxic wastes. Even scrupulous and responsible organizations indulge in the activity—mistakenly believing that
their wastes will be instantly and harmlessly dispersed in the
immense seas. Time and again the seas have demonstrated the
dubious nature of this belief. The lesson has still to be learned.
One day we may know enough about the movements of the
world ocean to confidently predict when and where it will be
safe to dump particular wastes in particular fashions, but that
day has yet to come. Drums of wastes confidently dropped in
deep (and therefore "safe") areas are continually reappearing
in fishermen's nets, on distant bathing beaches and on remote
stretches of sea floor being explored by aquanauts. As if this
were not bad enough, the containers are nearly always poorly
selected so that wherever they go they are likely to fall apart
(through corrosion or mechanical failure) long before the contents loose their potency.

It is disheartening that government agencies such as the
military should themselves engage in ocean dumping. This casts
doubts on their credibility when they attempt to prevent others
from doing likewise. The German military started dumping
cannisters of mustard gas in the Baltic just after the first world
war, and the Baltic has since received innumerable other cannisters of toxic military wastes. There have been many incidents in which fishermen have had to be hospital-treated after
taking on board leaking cannisters which fouled their nets. The
West German ministry of defense was eventually, in 1970, pres-
sured into sending divers into the Baltic to locate second world
war poison gas dumps. The U.S. military scandalized environmentalists when in the same year, it dumped enormous quantities of nerve-gas rockets and other obsolete munitions into
the Atlantic Ocean. (The nerve gas could have been chemically
disposed of on land.) It is probable that the containers will already have imploded, due to the high pressures at the depths
at which they were dumped, and that the gases will have escaped into surrounding sea water. Government scientists cal-

culated that a "mere" three cubic kilometers of sea water would be rendered toxic, but such predictions are more than a little spurious considering how little is known of deep-water movements and of susceptibilities of life in the depths. The British government was quick to decry the dumping publicly but few people took any notice as the British navy had been secretly dumping nerve gas into the ocean for some years. The bad publicity did eventually stir the U.S. government to suspend plans for further similar dumpings of obsolete munitions.

Studies by the United States government show that its own dumping activities pale before those of American industry. The first extensive report to be made on dumping in any area of the world ocean was made by the government in 1968. The report showed that 48 million tons of wastes were dumped in the oceans around the U.S. in 1968 and that 29 million dollars was spent on that dumping. Dumping was found to have increased fourfold in twenty years and showed no signs of abating. A study of the North Sea, made in the same year, showed that the Dutch alone poured in 3,600 tons of sulphuric acid and 750,000 tons of sulphur dioxide each year. The West Germans were found to be dumping 375 tons per day of sulphuric acid, 200,000 tons per year of gypsum, 750 tons per day of iron sulphate, 40 tons per month of chlorinated hydrocarbons, and 40 to 50 tons per month of polyethylene. The amounts will have increased since then and were probably greater at the time anyway—much dumping is clandestine. Fishermen are finding it worthwhile to take aboard illicit cargoes of toxin which they then dump. Fellow fishermen whose nets are ruined by the cannisters and whose livelihood is threatened by decreasing stocks of fish must be resentful of the whole exercise. Senator Gaylord Nelson said of the American report: "The Corps of Engineers confirmed that no one really knows how many people are dumping what kinds of wastes into the oceans." On the other hand most dumping is respectable big business. Specialist companies have sprung up to serve the increasing demand and some have even built or converted vessels solely for dumping.

Dumping is slowly being brought under control. Governments

which were themselves dumping just a year or so ago are now banding together to ban all dumping within their territorial waters, and some have actually cooperated to stop dumping beyond territorial waters. The first major international agreement to prevent dumping from ships and planes was signed in February 1972. The agreement was initiated by Norway (a nation which does little dumping but a lot of fishing) and covers the Northeast Atlantic; it embraces a wide range of toxic substances and is worded in a wide manner so that new chemical compounds will be able to be banned when they appear. It is an extremely encouraging agreement which could lead both to other regional international agreements and to the control of pollution from other sources (such as sewage outfalls and pipelines). Penalties for infringing the agreement will be severe but the exact steps to be taken to detect violations have yet to be clarified.

The control of dumping will only be effective when it is accompanied by legislation to control discharges from land into rivers and into the air. Air pollution is an area ripe both for tighter laws and for technological innovations which make it profitable to discharge clean gases into the atmosphere. The heavy metals are being depleted very rapidly, and mineral resources of silver, mercury, lead and zinc will probably all be exhausted by 1990. If mercury could be recovered from the gases produced by the combustion of fossil fuels, two birds would be killed with one stone (mercury resources may well be exhausted in the early eighties).

A significant proportion of the lead in the air is thought to come from petrol containing "antiknock" compounds. Petrol companies are reluctant to admit to this possibility and are actively obstructing attempts to bring in laws to restrict lead emissions from cars in North America and Western Europe. They will inevitably be defeated but it is a shame they have not seen fit to use their immense resources to make greater scientific contributions to the investigation of lead in the environment. The Russian and Japanese governments are already controlling the lead content of petrol and AMOCO is marketing lead-free petrol in some of its petrol stations in the United States. The problem is heightened by the fact that reductions in lead increase emissions of other noxious substances, and this will only be avoided when car manufacturers produce cars with smaller engines. This could very easily be done but would probably diminish profits.

Many attempts are being made to bring about a world-wide ban on the discharge of mercury into air and water. This would give scientists some time to determine how much mercury is being introduced by man into the environment and how much damage it does. Once such information is available it should be possible to instigate precise controls. A similar ban on cadmium might be even more useful but there are few signs that a ban on either will materialise in the near future.

As long as international controls are feeble or nonexistent, we can expect an increased burden on the seas. However effective national controls may be, they will not protect the world ocean if potential polluters are free to move their industries to impoverished countries. African leaders are beginning to worry about what they term "exported pollution." Japanese business leaders are known to be planning to make such moves. This will present terrible dilemmas to governments badly in need of money and jobs but dependent on their rivers and seas for their fish protein.

Even if international controls are ultimately put into effect there will be the occasional disastrous accident. When one single tanker of phenol came off a Danish road early in 1972 and spilled its contents we were treated to a foretaste of things to come. The tanker skidded off a slippery road, smashed into a water-tower and overturned. The driver, who later became ill, managed to stagger to the local village. The 200 local inhabitants were promptly evacuated and the village was sealed off. The waterworks was closed and water had to be taken into neighboring communities by lorry. It proved impossible to penetrate the fumes to the tanker and cool the phenol down until it formed a thick liquid. As the days went by it transpired that what had started as a road crash had developed into an environmental catastrophe. Dead fish were found floating in the local rivers and farmers worried that their soil might be irreversibly contaminated. Soil tests confirmed their worst suspicions and an enormous tonnage of soil had to be rapidly removed from the fields and replaced by uncontaminated topsoil. The entire stock of a nearby trout farm was killed off and filled seventy-two pools with their bodies. The waterworks was found to be so contaminated that it could never be used again. Some days later fish began to die off the coast some miles away. The numbers built up until a stretch fifteen miles long was covered with rotting fish. The Danish government and the public were deeply shocked by the incident and immediately set about improving their preparations for a repeat incident.

Other countries would do well to heed the Danish warning and to take a close look at their own state of preparedness. However stringent a country's laws may be accidents will happen. Specially trained teams should be on constant standby always ready to respond quickly to alarms.

The dumping of industrial wastes does not have to be a negative affair in which one is solely concerned with minimizing the damage being done. Some industrial wastes could actually be of benefit to the marine environment and to the life which inhabits it. Artificial reefs have been constructed off the coast of California by the careful dumping of scrapped cars. The cars provide shelter from predators and soon become encrusted with a thick coating of algae, barnacles and sea anemones. The variety of fish and plant life in the area can be increased in a matter of years.

Positive thinking about wastes is long overdue. We tend to talk about pollution and dirt rather than waste, but every piece of industrial material that is lost to the environment is waste. The Chinese have developed this approach to a laudable extent. As well as returning their organic wastes to the soil they are careful to conserve every last scrap of material produced as a by-product of industrial processes. Communes and individual workers make fertilizers, for example, out of nitrogenous wastes from chemical factories.

Much research is being carried out in the West to see how the waste heat of power stations could be put to effective use. Existing stations were sited without much thought being given to the effects of discharged cooling water. Most discharge their water into the nearest river or sea, but none are positioned so that the river or sea will derive maximum benefit. Most actually damage the bodies of water into which they discharge their coolants. Studies of Biscayne Bay revealed that heated water discharged into it from a power station had simplified the pattern of life. Seaweeds and grasses had been replaced by simpler, less productive blue-green algae; fewer species were present in smaller numbers.

Increasing power demands mean that power plants will be springing up all along the coast, and seven United States power companies plan to construct a power plant that would actually be anchored at sea. The waste hot water from power stations would be best used to heat homes but this is still a rare step and it is more probable that the power stations of the near future will pump the water straight back into the sea. Given this approach it is to be hoped that more countries follow the approach of Sweden whose government has a complex computer model to help it plan the siting of future stations. Two new power stations are due to be commissioned soon and another dozen may follow the next decade. If these were haphazardly sited their cumulative effect could be disastrous. On the other hand, careful siting could be beneficial to marine life and lead to increased fish yields. (Naturally the latter would also be dependent on the careful control of all the other inputs which are currently damaging the Baltic.)

There are plans afoot to build twenty more power stations on the Rhine in the next few years, and other large rivers are bound to receive similar attentions as sources of cooling water and receptacles of heated discharge water. As it is not possible to resite estuaries the consequences are disturbing to contemplate. One of the best positive solutions to the problem of the disposal of waste water is that future power stations should be sited so that they can have large cooling ponds adjacent to them. These could be used for breeding fish and for recreational uses such as sports, fishing, boating and swimming. Environmentalists of the future could increase their credibility considerably if they tried, every time they found themselves forced to make negative suggestions ("We don't want your power station here"), to publicize positive alternative suggestions—such as those that already exist for the disposal of hot water.

The Black Death

7

Many people equate marine pollution with oil pollution. A series of major disasters right round the world has brought to public attention the scale on which man is releasing oil into the seas, but such accidental spills represent less than 10 percent of the 2 million metric tons of oil that man introduces directly into the world ocean every year. The other 90 percent results from the normal day-to-day operations of tankers, other ships, refineries, petrochemical plants and offshore oil wells, and from the disposal of industrial oils.

In addition to the oil he dumps directly into the seas, man introduces at least another 10 million tons via the rivers and the atmosphere. Twenty thousand gallons of used oil from cars and other machinery have been estimated to enter the sewage system of Schenectady, New York, every month. Extrapolations from this figure suggest that as much as half a billion gallons of oil enter the sewage systems of the United States every month from petrol stations and garages alone. A survey carried out under the auspices of the Massachusetts Institute of Technology in 1970 showed that spent crankcase oil may be a greater source of oil pollution than all marine activities such as the transportation and drilling of oil.

Another subtle source that could easily be neglected is petroleum that is lost entirely by evaporation in the transfers from refinery to lorry-tanker, from lorry-tanker to petrol station holding tank, from holding tank to car petrol tank, and while standing in petrol tanks and carburetors. Calculations show that these losses represent, in the United States, 2½ percent by volume of the total annual production. It seems probable that a large proportion of the evaporated fraction comes down over the ocean and contaminates surface waters. It is conservatively estimated that only 16 percent of the 90 millions tons of evaporated petroleums from all sources which are introduced into the air annually finally enters the seas. If this is even a slight underestimate the consequences to our conceptions of oceanic oil pollution are enormous.

In the course of five years estimates of the quantities of oil in the seas have risen by several orders of magnitude. Whatever the precise amount, there is at least as great a quantity of hydrocarbons in the oceans from oils as from living matter (hydrocarbons are, next to water, the main constituent of living organisms). Man has introduced far more oil into the seas than he has any other substance. Thor Heyerdahl's report that tar globules, derived from dumped oil, are to be found right across the Atlantic Ocean has since been confirmed by scientists trawling plankton nets in the surface waters of the ocean. Tar globules constitute, on average, over 20 percent of the material collected. Trawls in the Sargasso Sea, a remote region of the Atlantic infrequently visited by ships, caught in the plankton nets three times as large a quantity of oily lumps as of the Sargassum seaweed which gives the sea its name.

Marine oil pollution shows every sign of increasing in the near future. World oil consumption has doubled in the past decade and is confidently expected to double again by the end of the next decade. The forces involved in this inexorable doubling process are enormous and should not be underestimated. Multinational petro-chemical industries, and the car manufacturers who are dependent on them, are the principal economic forces on the planet. They have gained their power because of public acceptance of their products. If people did not buy cars, plastics, inorganic fertilizers, electricity and other goods made from or by petroleum, then those companies would not exist. But a massive inertia—born of a combination of consumer habits, rising expections, profit maximization and advertising—counteracts any attempts to strike at the heart of oil pollution: oil consumption.

It is not yet possible to receive a sympathetic audience if one points out that oil is a finite resource that will start to run out before the end of the century and that we ought therefore to curtail our consumption drastically, so as to slow down the rate of depletion and ease the transition to a technology not based on petroleum. If anyone suggests abandoning petroleum as a source of electric power, as a fuel for transport or as a raw material for the chemical industry, he comes up against a dispiriting wall of public opinion and vested interests. Given the assumption that the industrialized countries will continue to burn up the planet's oil reserves at an accelerating rate, one can only look at the likely consequences and suggest how damage might be minimized.

An increasing percentage of the world's oil production is expected to come from offshore oil wells. This results from the depletion of reserves on land, demands for higher prices from the traditional oil producing countries and the proximity of the undersea oil fields to industrialized nations. Drilling technology has still not developed to the extent that spillage can be avoided, and the blowout of oil wells in the Santa Barbara Channel off California showed how devastating oil extraction accidents under the sea can be. Scots and Norwegian fishermen are extremely worried that the development of the North Sea oil field will affect their catches. Another point is that, while all existing offshore oil wells are situated in comparatively shallow waters, the Lockheed Aircraft Corporation has developed devices which will enable oil companies to drill at depths of 300 meters and more; if drilling at this depth becomes feasible in the near future, large new areas of untapped oil would be opened up and one could expect increased dangers of leakage.

Transporting the oil from the fields to the consumer will probably become yet more dangerous to marine life as supertankers become more predominant. The calamitous grounding of the *Torrey Canyon* in the English Channel pales before the mayhem that would ensue from the destruction of one of the half-million-ton dinosaur tankers that will soon be in operation. Although the odds for collision may perhaps be reduced by the lesser number of tankers that will be traveling the seas, their difficult maneuverability, the increased density of other sea freighterage traffic and the size of collision target supertankers offer make it probable that disasters will continue to happen. A report made for the United States government states: "A single spill from one of the new large tankers could add 20 percent to the amount of petroleum entering the oceans (directly) in a single year." Already three of the handful of supertankers in operation suffered mysterious explosions in the month of December in 1969. The oil companies concerned have since conducted copious inquiries to determine the cause of the explosions but have yet to find it. It is suspected that static electricity may have built up as the tankers were being washed and that it sparked the gases left in the empty ships. Rather than suspend the operation of supertankers, the major oil companies are committed to rapidly expanding their fleets of them.

Difficult transportation problems await British Petroleum and other companies hoping to extract oil from a large field discovered on the North Slope in Alaska. Such enormous sums of money are at stake that there is little hope that Eskimos, fishermen and environmentalists will succeed in affecting the exploitation of the field. They are currently engaged, amongst other things, in attempting to prevent the oil being piped to the South Alaskan coast for shipping to the United States. Their chances of success are regrettably low. The U.S. Department of the Interior recognizes that there will be spillages but does not seem too worried at the prospect.

The Russians have already had unfortunate experiences in their efforts to pipe oil in freezing temperatures. A report in

Pravda stated that the steel pipeline had been unable to withstand the stresses caused by the low temperature outside and the high internal temperature of the heated oil. The breakage was considered a serious threat to the sturgeon fishing grounds of the Caspian Sea and to the fertile bottom lands of nearby collective and state farms, Oil is a far greater environmental threat in the polar regions: low temperatures slow down considerably the rate of evaporation and degradation of Arctic oil, and any areas where life was wiped out would take a long time to be recolonized, due to the slow rates of growth and reproduction in a cold climate and also to the fact that microscopic Arctic organisms (unlike those in other regions) do not have stages in their cycles where they travel long distances. Furthermore, Arctic ecosystems are simpler in structure, consisting of large numbers of a few species. This makes them unstable and vulnerable to assaults which affect just one or two species. Another vast oil field, three times the size of the one on the North Slope, has since been discovered under large areas of Siberia, Arctic Canada and Alaska.

Indirect introductions of oil to the marine environment are expected to increase at the same rate as consumption—they should double by 1980. Unless we take much more effective action than we are taking at present, the total amount of petroleum products in the seas will quickly reach staggering dimensions. Their effects cannot be predicted as we are still largely ignorant of the nonlethal effects of widespread low concentrations of oil residues in sea water, but as new information comes in the picture gets worse and worse.

Most available information was collected as a result of observations of oil slicks. As only a small fraction of marine oil is derived from slicks these findings are far from the complete picture but they are still very useful. Oil is black, sticky and to many people an archetypal "dirty" industrial pollutant. This view conveniently neglects the fact that oil is a "natural" substance formed millions of years ago by the compression of marine microorganisms. Since that time a small amount has seeped back into the ocean "naturally" but there is no evidence that this has been sufficiently widespread for marine organisms to adapt special protective measures, and few of them are capable of dealing with the physical and chemical properties of an oil slick.

Although the press only bothers to report the occasional large oil slick, every day sees at least one small slick being formed somewhere in the world ocean. One such small slick happened to form near the Woods Hole Oceanographic Institution in Massachusetts. An interdisciplinary group of scientists seized the opportunity to study the long-term effects of small-scale oil pollution. They spent many months observing changes in the sea water and the organisms that lived in it and came to some disturbing conclusions. They knew that petroleum oils differ in composition from those occurring in living organisms but were not too sure how important a threat that difference posed to marine life. They concluded that "oil is much more persistent and destructive to marine organisms and to man's food resources than scientists had thought." They discovered that many of the more toxic hydrocarbons did not evaporate as readily as was expected but found their way into organisms and into the bottom sediments. Once inside the organisms they build up in food chains in much the same way as other persistent toxins (the chlorinated hydrocarbons and heavy metals, for example).

Oil-laden sediments can be moved by bottom currents and contaminate areas away from the immediate vicinity of the spill. In this way, a single relatively small spill can lead to chronic destructive pollution of a large area. The scientists at Woods Hole found that "massive, immediate destruction of marine life" occurred offshore during the first few days after the spill. Many species of fish, shellfish, worms, crabs, other crustaceans and invertebrates were affected. Lobsters and bottom-living fish were the only dead animals to be washed up on neighboring beaches but trawls made in ten feet of water soon after the accident showed that 95 percent of the animals recovered were dead and that others were dying. Examination of the bottom sediments revealed many dead snails, clams and crustaceans. Evidence of further marked destruction was found in the tidal stretches of local rivers and on salt marshes which would otherwise have been exceptionally rich in life and biologically productive. In the most heavily polluted areas of the salt marshes almost every animal was killed, and in the rest fish, crabs, shellfish and other invertebrates were killed in large numbers. Most of the dead animals decayed within a few days and there was little visible evidence of the oil. A passerby would have concluded that the episode was over, but scientific analysis showed this assessment to be far from the truth.

The scientists applied advanced techniques of chemical analysis which helped them to "fingerprint" the various characteristics of the spilled oil. Before these techniques were applied, it had been assumed that visual observation of the apparent disappearance of a spill indicate that the oil had evaporated or been completely broken down by bacteria. Chemical analysis showed this to be a false assumption. Eight months after the spill, oil essentially unaltered in characteristics was still being recovered from the sediments of the most heavily polluted areas. After a year the fingerprint pattern of oil from all locations showed signs of change but in the sediments the bacteria had only attacked the least toxic elements. The oil residues slowly spread and within a year polluted an area ten times greater than that immediately after the accident. The oil spill closed the area to the harvesting of shellfish which proved very effective at taking up oil. Juvenile shellfish were sterilized by the oil and adults had an unpleasant oily taste. The taste disappeared when the shellfish were placed in clean water but it was found that much of the oil stays in the animals for a long time—possibly the rest of their lives. In the second shellfish season after the spill an even larger area of fishery had to be closed due to the spread of the oil residues. One and a half years after the incident the original animal populations had not been reestablished, except for a few species of pollution-resistant organisms. Small spills such as this occur every day in the coastal regions of the world and are a far more significant source of chronic pollution with serious biological consequences than the very occasional big spills.

The spill just described consisted of fuel oil rather than the crude oil carried around in supertankers. Much inshore pollution probably consists of fuel oil, and other studies have shown that it has had even more devastating effects in other spills. When the *Tampico* ran aground off the west coast of the United States, only four species of attached plants and two species of bottom-living animals survived. Crude unrefined oil is much thicker than fuel oil and acts quite differently. The immediate widespread killing of animals and plants which followed the *Torrey Canyon* disaster was a result of the physical thickness of the film of oil which smothered them, but chemical effects of crude oil pollution have also been noted. Shellfish are rendered unpalatable, their growth and feeding slow down and they may slowly starve to death if their filters become sufficiently clogged. Fish can be affected in many ways—ranging from cancers of the skin to disequilibrium. Chemical messages carried through sea water are important to fish in their search for prey, sexual partners and areas in which to spawn; the presence of oil can interfere drastically with the transmission of such chemical messages. Another form of seafood was destroyed when 5,000 tons of crude oil escaped from the wreck of a tanker off the coast of Japan. The spill caused an enormous amount of ecological damage and wiped out huge beds of cultured seaweeds that are an important part of the Japanese diet. Oil spills are particularly dangerous to birds and have decimated the populations of many species in the coastal regions of the Northeast Atlantic. Twenty-five thousand birds died as a result of the grounding of the *Torrey Canyon,* but the Nature Conservancy of Britain estimated that the same number of birds died from routine oil pollution around Britain's coasts in the four months from November 1969 to February 1970. Sea birds are easily killed by oil pollution because once their plumage is oiled they cannot fly and are doomed to drown or starve. Their attempts to clean their plumage by scraping off and swallowing oil probably lead to disruption of the digestive and reproductive systems. As most of the species affected (for instance diving birds) do not reproduce quickly, the regular exposure of their numbers to oil pollution can have a devastating effect. Most of Britain's coastal birds are in decline and all over the world reports come in of species faced with extinction. Even the Cape of Good Hope in South Africa receives so much regular oil pollution that the jackass penguin is faced with imminent extinction. The removal of predatory sea birds from the tops of marine food chains is probably having untold ecological consequences.

Oil spills in tropical seas are known to have significantly disrupted the stability of coral communities. These productive and complex systems have elaborate stabilizing controls which had been thought to be adequate to deal with pollution. Studies of reefs and atolls covered by crude oil show that they were badly damaged and will take a long time to return to a stable state, if indeed they ever do.

The effects of low level background oil pollution in coastal and noncoastal areas have hardly been studied. Oil slicks are closer to home and of greater public interest—both good reasons for attention. Nonetheless there has been a certain neglect of the ecological consequences of the low-level oil pollution which is found throughout the world ocean. The tarry lumps which Thor Heyerdahl discovered are still comparatively understudied. It would also be interesting to learn more of synergistic relationships between oil and other pollutants. It is known that DDE, PCBs and other chlorinated hydrocarbons dissolve readily in oil and high concentrations of them are found in surface films of oil. Does the same apply to the tar lumps? Carcinogens (cancer-causing agents) have been found in crude oil: it is possible that they are passed on to man when he eats fish and other seafood contaminated with oil, though it is not yet known whether this does or does not happen. Considering the accelerating rate at which we are adding to the oil already in the seas, it is high time that scientists were given the money to find out.

Attempts to control the influx of oil into the seas have been made for over two decades. These have concentrated on preventing spillage from the routine operations of tankers and were initially motivated by the knowledge that lost oil is lost money. The first move was to stop losses through the hulls of the riveted tankers that were in use just after the second world war. Each tanker was held together by hundreds of thousands of rivets, many of which were loosened by storms and leaked oil to the sea. This problem was solved when riveted hulls were replaced by welded hulls, but losses through leaking rivets could not compare to those which resulted from ballasting and the cleaning of tanks.

Ballasting involves taking on sea water (usually equivalent in weight to one third of the oil cargo) so that the empty tanker rides low enough in the water to be seaworthy on its return journey from refinery to oil field or pipeline terminal. During the return journey the tanks have to be washed out, and as their total surface area amounts to some acres even in a fairly small tanker, it is not surprising that the cleaning operations remove a fair weight of oil (approximately 0.3 percent of the original cargo). It used to be commonplace to wash the tanks out at sea and to discharge the waste oil overboard. The first major step to curtail this practice was the International Convention for the Prevention of Pollution of the Sea by Oil which was concluded in 1954. This Convention attempted to diminish coastal pollution by stipulating that the oily wastes should be concentrated before discharge and that they should be dumped at least a hundred miles from the coast. This meant that the same weight of oil entered the seas—it just did so from different points, and often those points corresponded closely to areas of the continental shelves where fish had their breeding grounds. Oil was still washed up on beaches in large amounts and the public continued to complain.

The first real breakthrough in the problem of tank cleaning

and ballasting was the development of the load-on-top system. In this system the oily water resulting from tank cleaning is put into a settling tank where the oil and water separate out, and the separated water is slowly removed. The next problem is disposing of the recovered oil. It might be thought that this oil (a substance often lovingly labeled "black gold") would be jealously guarded and regarded as an asset. When the tanker puts into port it soon learns otherwise. The greater weight than that of a completely empty tanker means that the harbormaster will feel entitled to extra dues, the customs officer may feel that you are importing oil and will charge you accordingly, and the company chartering your vessel may not want you to mix the waste oil with the new load of oil. In many instances it has been found easier to discharge the problem at sea. If the minor financial problems could be ironed out the load-on-top system could work tomorrow. Every oil terminal would have to have a reservoir for receiving the waste oils. The majority of oil terminals that are owned by oil companies have such facilities but 20 percent of the world tanker fleet has yet to adopt the load-on-top system. Most of the errant tankers are old ones, independently owned and solely concerned with maximizing profits on each journey. The only realistic way to curb their activities would be to make it profitable to switch to load-on-top (or unprofitable not to) and to ensure that every terminal had onshore facilities for taking waste oils.

A great deal of very expensive research is at present being conducted into the mystery of supertanker explosions. Insurance brokers the world over became so reluctant to insure supertankers at any price that something had to be done. One result of the research is a long list of factors which most probably do not increase the risk of explosion and a short list of modifications to tanker design and to cleaning operations that might minimize the risks. If, as seems possible, the build-up of static electricity is involved, it will be necessary to reduce the size of individual compartments in the new supertankers. The hull of a supertanker is divided into self-contained compartments, each of which takes on its own load. One tank of a 300,000-ton tanker may contain about 24,000 tons of oil—compared to the 16,000 tons carried in an entire second world war tanker. Steps are now being taken by the International Maritime Consultative Organization (IMCO) to limit the sizes of individual compartments. This will be extremely expensive for the supertanker operators but it will both reduce the risk of explosion and limit the amount of oil which would escape in a collision or grounding.

Collisions become increasingly probable as densities of shipping traffic increase. The situation is already critical in the English Channel, the North Sea and the Mediterranean. In the Channel it has become necessary to introduce a one-way traffic separation scheme. Speed limits related to the size and maneuverability of vessels and to conditions of visibility would also help, as the most common failures arise from ships attempting to navigate areas of high traffic density in conditions of low visibility at too high a speed, Obviously improved standards of navigational training would not go amiss.

Measures to reduce routine and accidental direct dumping of oil into the world ocean are of course to be welcomed but the major problem remains the indirect influx of millions of tons of oil. This enormously important area is disgracefully under-researched and consequently very little can be done to control it. However, one important source that is amenable to change is waste oil from petrol-driven transport. While it may be over-optimistic to pray for an immediate switch to cleaner methods of transport, it seems reasonable to expect two devices to be taken up soon which would cheaply and quickly diminish oil outputs from this source. Thanks to a cheap new filtration system it is now possible to convert any vehicle so that it cleans and recycles its lubricating oil—avoiding the disposal of dirty oil every few thousands miles. Another simple device is a small oil separation tank which can be fitted into the waste-pipe system of vehicle workshops and other places where oil changes are frequently made. The problem of reducing evaporation of petroleum hydrocarbons from vehicle fuels is a more intractable one—perhaps it is amenable to greater care rather than gadgetry.

It is highly unlikely that any controls could completely eliminate the occasional accident. Future planning must take this into account and improve methods for dealing with localized oil spills. At present there is not one satisfactory system. Huge sums are being spent in the search for a wonder clean-up method and many organizations possess expensive equipment to which they ascribe unlikely powers.

One approach is to burn the oil. This was attempted in the case of the *Torrey Canyon* which was bombarded with napalm. The spectacular blaze which ensued merely transferred a fraction of the contaminants into the atmosphere—only to return to the seas at the first fall of rain. This is clearly a crude, unsatisfactory method of disposal but it may well be preferable to some of the other methods tried. Another *Torrey Canyon* approach was the widespread application of detergents (or "oil dispersants"). Subsequent analysis showed that these were probably as toxic to sea life as the oil they were expected to disperse. Soon nontoxic dispersants were developed but the very success of these was their failing. They act by breaking slicks down into minute droplets which disperse in the sea water, and this has the undesirable effect of causing a greater volume of sea water to be contaminated faster. It also greatly increases the surface area of oil in the water as millions of minute droplets have a far greater surface area than one big drop. This increases the rate at which the toxic elements of the oil reach sea water and increases the odds on contact with marine organisms.

Any successful method of dealing with oil pollution must rapidly do one of two things: remove the oil or break it down into harmless chemical elements. Physical redisposition of the oil within the sea can have little more than a cosmetic effect. The very best method would be to remove every last drop of oil from the sea water. This is a remote—but economically as well as environmentally desirable—aim. Steps in that direction include the use of spotter planes to locate slicks as soon as possible after their formation, and it may soon be possible to use radar to do this on days of poor visibility. Once spotted, the slick can be contained by booms and the oil pumped into an empty tanker. This all sounds fine until one considers the time factor. Even if weather conditions are good and the waves have not dispersed the slick significantly before action can be taken, there is the difficult problem of getting an appropriate length of boom and tankers to the slick at high speed. The longer the slick stays in the water the greater the damage it does and the more of it eludes the pumps. Very few high performance booms are available and, even if they were better organized, it is unlikely that they could cope with more than a fraction of the incidents that occur daily. It is sadly true that current action amounts to little more than the cleaning of beaches.

Until oil removal techniques are much improved and are taken off the drawing boards and put into practice, one of the most interesting developments is the creation of mixed cultures of microorganisms which eat up oil and reduce it to basic organic chemical elements that can be used as nutrients by other living things in the sea. These can never be the ultimate solution, as biological processes are unable to keep up with the pace at which the contaminants in slicks spread into the wider marine environment. Also, the example of eutrophication and deoxygenation caused by organic wastes shows us that the localized introduction of large quantities of nutrients into the marine environment is not necessarily a good idea.

In recent years many economic steps have been taken to ensure that nations, groups and individuals affected by oil spills are compensated for the damage done to their interests. This is clearly an excellent idea which should be encouraged, but it must be made clear that we never want a situation where a tanker operator can decide that he would rather spill and pay up than go through any complications involved in not spilling.

Likewise it would be sad if a poor community or nation decided that it was prepared to tolerate oil pollution so long as it made a substantial income from the situation. Many industrialists on land have decided they would rather pay fines than stop polluting rivers and lakes. This is a fool's paradise that we cannot afford—on environmental grounds. Money cannot pay for damage done to the marine ecosystem and no such pretence should be fostered. Negligent operators of oil tankers should experience the full brunt of public opprobium; they should be deprived of any opportunity of repeating their offense; and they should not only compensate for the damage they do but also pay for the clean-up, make a contribution towards the costs of monitoring the marine environment for oil damage, and help finance research into the many unknown areas of oil pollution.

The many complications involved in an appreciation of the problems of oil pollution were well summarized in an editorial of the *Marine Pollution Bulletin*:

> The fact is that even after a decade of serious investigation, great publicity and much international and national legislation, we still have very incomplete ideas about oil pollution. What we have discovered is that the solution to one problem raises new problems, and that changing technology constantly changes the nature of the problems. If this is true of our best known pollutant in the sea, we cannot expect that problems of pollutants we have only just discovered will be solved at the stroke of a pen. We have a long haul in front of us and the sooner that is realized the better.
>
> Let's hope there is time.

Radioactive Wastes

8

Radioactive wastes evoke even more emotional responses than toxic chemical wastes. The passionate debate between proponents and opponents of increased human use of nuclear power usually centers around those aspects which are least researched—in particular the paths of radioactive materials in the environment and their cumulative biological impacts. Enormous pressures are building up which make nuclear power increasingly important to man: planners often find themselves in situations where nuclear generation of power appears to be the only option open to them and become extremely impatient with anyone who suggests that it is too dangerous to implement.

Apologists for the unthinking expansion of nuclear technology point out that human activities have only added a small fraction to the natural background radiation from cosmic rays, radioactive rocks and certain substances in the human body (especially potassium). The radioactive wastes released so far by man to the marine environment probably amount to less than 3 percent of the background radiation from natural sources. It is argued that our contribution is so small and that living organisms are so accustomed to natural radiation that we should not worry too much. The homino-centric logic of technology bolsters this reassurance with the observation that levels of releases are scrupulously controlled so that even people maximally exposed do not receive a dangerous dose and that therefore all other living things must be safe too.

The apologists may turn out to be right. At present there is not enough evidence to substantiate or contradict their claims. Very little research has been done on the long-term effects of low levels of radiation and much argument is based on hunches and suspicions. There are some signs that nuclear technologists might be indulging in wishful thinking about the biological consequences of their actions.

It is all very well to point out that radiation is emitted naturally from certain rocks on the earth's surface, but one must also show that it does not have adverse effects on humans and other living things living on those rocks. Studies of the inhabitants of the Brazilian coastal town of Guarapary, which lies on radioactive rocks, show that there is a statistically significant excess of genetic aberrations over levels found in non-radioactive areas. Other research on the Deccan plateau of India and in New York State correlates natural background radiation with possible high levels of genetic damage and a high incidence of diseases associated with radiation. Two scientists, Gofman and Tamplin, who were working for the United States Atomic Energy Commission conducted extensive research into safe levels of exposure to radiation for humans and came to the conclusion that these were very near to natural levels and that man should release far less radiation to the environment. These findings did not fit into AEC plans, so the two scientists were subjected to an incredible barrage of bureaucratic harassment to hinder further embarrassing research. Little convincing counterargument was produced but the scientists were unfortunately goaded into responses as hysterical as those of the AEC. The dispute did little to inform the public of the questions at issue.

Other doubts about the wisdom of blindly adding to background radiation are based on differences between naturally produced radiation and that produced by man. Marine and other organisms have adapted over a period of millions of years to a fairly narrow range of radioactive substances, from a limited range of places where they are present at fairly constant levels. Man has suddenly introduced a whole new range of radioactive materials and is releasing them at comparatively high levels in areas that have received little radiation before. Natural geophysical processes and biological processes cause even greater concentrations in individual organisms and increase the risks of damage. Marine organisms are shielded by sea water from much natural radiation and are therefore less accustomed to it than terrestrial organisms. Marine food chains are also longer and more concentrative than terrestrial ones, so the odds on a dangerous dose are that much greater.

The radiations of interest to biologists are "ionizing radiations." These are invisible electromagnetic waves and subatomic particles which travel at very high speeds and have the ability to penetrate living tissue. In their passage through living tissue they knock electrons off atoms and cause the latter to become charged and therefore chemically active. This activity is usually incompatible with the normal functioning of the cell in which it occurs: the very smallest doses of radiation cause changes to cells and large doses can kill them almost instantaneously. In a limited sense—we do not know precisely how limited—all radiation is dangerous. The degree of danger from any one source is a function not only of the quantity of radiation it emits but also of its longevity and of the susceptibilities of the organisms it contacts. The length of time for which a radioactive source continues to emit varies considerably, but all radioactive substances "decay," turning into stable nonradioactive forms as they lose matter or energy in the form of ionizing radiation. The rate of decay is customarily expressed as the "half-life" of a substance—that is, the time taken for half its radiation to be released. (The half-life is *not* half the time for which the substance continues to emit radiation. As it loses energy it emits more and more slowly, so that the radiation is, as it were, spread out over an indefinitely long period, for much of which it is at immeasurably low levels.) Half-lives vary considerably, from a few seconds to millions of years. Organisms, too, vary considerably in their reactions to ionizing radiations. When considering chemical toxins it is assumed that closely related species will be affected in similar ways by the same quantity of a given toxin, and this was once assumed to be the case for radioactive materials as well. It was shown to be false with the repeated discovery of very closely related species which reacted entirely differently to identical doses. A Russian scientist, G. G. Polikarpov, made the most complete survey ever undertaken of the effects of man's releases of radioactive wastes into the marine environment, the results of his work being first published in 1964 in a book entitled *The Radioecology of Aquatic Organisms*. In this book Polikarpov stated categorically: "further (radioactive) contamination of the sea is inadmissible." Since that time contamination has increased considerably and little evidence has been produced to counter the charge of its inadmissibility.

The first large-scale human release of radioactivity to the environment came from the use and testing of nuclear weapons. When a nuclear device is exploded on or above the surface of the earth, large quantities of radioactive dust are blown up towards the upper atmosphere. The portion of that dust which slowly drifts back to the surface of the earth is known as fallout. More than 200 different radioactive materials can be released in one explosion and their distribution is difficult to predict. By the time some of the materials reach the ground they have already lost much of their radioactivity, but other materials take a long time to come down and even longer to decay, so that an explosion can have dangerous effects long after it takes place. The delay can be modified by biological activity. Thus in 1971 there was a sudden upsurge in the incidence of cancer among people exposed to the atom bomb which destroyed Hiroshima at the end of the second world war.

It is thought that more fallout per unit area is deposited over the oceans than over the land masses, but there is, however, dispute even over basic points such as this. Different measurements have shown the rate of deposition over the seas to be variously several times greater, 50 percent greater, and in one case less, than it is over land. In addition to being deposited directly into the ocean, fallout is slowly leached off land surfaces into sea water. Much of the river-borne material is deposited in the sediments of estuaries, due to the chemical processes induced when sea water meets fresh water.

The Nuclear Test Ban Treaty of 1963 significantly reduced radioactive emissions from the surface of the earth or above and therefore cut down the amount of fallout reaching the earth, but much fallout from before the treaty has yet to be deposited or leached into the ocean. The peak in the rate of emission is thought to have been reached about 1965. The French and Chinese are still engaged in above-surface testing of nuclear weapons and show little will to cease. Their contribution is negligible compared to that of previous testing by the governments of the United States and the Soviet Union, but it is still reprehensible.

The Russians and Americans have yet to reach agreement over the banning of underground testing of nuclear weapons (invalid technical excuses, concerning the problems of detecting illicit tests, are the main stumbling block to a total ban). Meanwhile the Americans have conducted a series of underground tests that may well be adding to the radioactive burden of the seas. A technical report on an underground test carried out on the Alaskan island of Amchitka in 1970 suggested that radioactive materials would take six years to reach the ocean. In the interim it will no doubt be argued that as no wide-scale deleterious effects have been detected so far it will be quite in order to continue testing. Such arguments could rebound if the report's predictions are fulfilled. Among other things, it predicts that once it has reached the ocean the radioactive waste will remain above maximum permissible levels for as long as sixty-six years.

France and China could be joined at any time by other nations wishing to develop international muscle at the expense of brain power. Periodic rumors that Israel, South Africa, India and other countries are on the verge of developing atomic weapons are circulated by the media, and sooner or later the rumors will come true. Countries with nuclear generating stations could soon develop the necessary hardware, as the technology is being continuously simplified. Some nuclear scientists have even made the alarming claim that private business, criminal or political groups could manufacture their own bombs. There is already enough fallout in the upper atmosphere to contaminate jet engine turbines to a dangerous extent (the British Overseas Airways Corporation has had to institute special procedures for overhauling jet engines), and there are other indications that we would be wise to prevent as soon as possible all releases of radioactive materials to the atmosphere. This entails more than stopping tests and the spread of nuclear power. Safety will have to be tightened up considerably. The crash of a bomber carrying nuclear weapons at Palomares in Spain could not be hushed up, but there is reason to believe that both the American and Russian governments have managed to conceal other incidents. Milton Leitenberg, writing in the American magazine *Environment,* commented that "there are reasons for believing that the total number of accidents involving nuclear weapon systems is significantly higher than the number officially announced." Increasing stockpiles of nuclear weaponry can only raise the odds on a large unconcealable accident.

Another potential source of fallout is the infant nuclear civil engineering industry. Many hair-raising and childishly megalomaniac schemes have been proposed to explode nuclear devices on or near the surface of the earth in order to create useful holes or movements of rock. So far there have been few explosions and they have all been relatively innocuous subterranean ones. At the end of 1971 the government of the Soviet Union revealed details of the detonation of an underground nuclear charge of "unprecedented force" to extinguish a fire that burned out of control for three years in a Central Asian natural gas field. The fire was successfully quelled and the field is once again in commercial production. No mention was made of the levels of radiation produced although the account contained this interesting passage: "A dusty haze rose over the desert. The orange-colored torch of the blazing well diminished, first slowly, then more rapidly, until it flickered and finally died out." Fallout is often described as "a dusty haze." This might explain why it took five years to get the economically important field back in production and to print any report in the press.

The most worrying schemes are the surface ones, though fortunately none of these have yet been carried out. One of the craziest was the proposal to blast a sea-level canal between the Atlantic and Pacific Oceans. Apart from the ecological arguments against the mixing of Pacific and Atlantic waters, investigation showed that quite unacceptable levels of radiation would be released. The idea was taken seriously enough to be studied by a United States presidential commission but was finally stopped. Other plans for surface explosions exist in Australia, and a private nuclear excavation company has been registered in Paris. Further adventures of the United States government are likely to be curbed by the economic problems it faces. Operation Plowshare, the grandiosely named originator of most American nuclear excavation plans, has had its finances drastically cut and is unlikely to do anything other than dream expensive dreams for some time. Information about the state of affairs in the Soviet Union is hard to come by, but it is known that the plan to join two enormous Arctic rivers, the Ob and the Yenisei, has finally been abandoned.

Fallout from atmospheric contamination is not the only human source of radioactive materials in the environment. Increasing amounts are coming from the wastes produced by the rapidly expanding nuclear power generation industry. It is predicted that production of electricity by nuclear plants will increase over fortyfold outside the Soviet block in the period 1968 to 1980. At the same time individual plants are expected to be enlarged until they are ten to twelve times the size of those in operation today. There is mounting concern that these increases will be bought at the cost of dangerous accidents.

There have already been one or two serious accidents. The first major mishap was the malfunction in 1957 of the Windscale plant which completely destroyed its number one pile and released more radioactivity into the atmosphere than fell on Hiroshima in 1945 after the explosion of an atomic bomb. An entirely fortuitous cloud inversion happened to carry the material upwards away from local inhabitants and dispersed it to add to the load of fallout already present in the upper atmosphere. In October 1966 the Enrico Fermi breeder reactor also went "critical." There were fears that measures taken to quiet the reactor down might misfire, causing a chain reaction similar to that in a nuclear weapon and threatening the lives of $1\frac{1}{2}$ million people. The incident was found to have been caused by the bad riveting of a small metal plate which had come loose and hindered the cooling system. Many accidents occur in the transportation of fuels for reactors and in the removal of their wastes. Forty percent of the accidents in the United States between 1960 and 1963 involved transportation.

Accidents norwithstanding, the greatest problem of the nuclear generation of power is the routine disposal of the low-level radioactive wastes it produces continuously. Nearly all reactors are at present situated on the coast or on a large body of water connected to the ocean, and routinely release small quantities of radioactivity to the aquatic environment. This represents the residue that cannot be processed for reuse as fuel or extracted in solid form for disposal in sealed containers. So far little evidence of damage resulting from this practice has been detected. This may be a function of our ignorance—or it may not.

The disposal of highly radioactive solid wastes leaves much to be desired. The wastes are usually placed in steel and concrete containers, but these rarely contain the expensive walling needed to prevent some radiations penetrating the containers and entering the environment. A United Nations publication *Marine Pollution—Potential for Catastrophe* rightly points out that "No one expects the containers to last forever, even those who make them." Reports have already come in from divers who have found broken containers on the sea bed. Many containers have been dumped in deep oceanic trenches in the mistaken belief that the oceans depths are immobile, but in fact there are earthquake shockwaves which pass through the sea floor and the water as well as powerful subsurface currents.

It is not known how much radioactive material has been deposited in containers in the sea, as the concentrations in individual containers are not known and as some users are "reluctant to identify themselves or the magnitude of their disposals." Economics has dictated that more wastes are now being disposed of on land, but one should not draw too much comfort from this tendency since many of the sites are ill chosen. There are too many incidents of burials in disused mine shafts liable to subsidence or in areas prone to earthquakes for there to be any confidence that existing controls are adequate.

Nuclear ships are another expanding source of marine radioactive wastes. Most of their routine discharges involve coolant sea water, but far greater amounts of radioactive material are contained in the used fuel elements which are normally taken ashore for reprocessing. Accidental sinkings can prevent this happening and cause significant contamination of the ocean. Two nuclear submarines, the *Thresher* and the *Scorpion,* are known to have sunk. Others could follow. Also, as supplies of uranium fuel dry up, the existing fission reactors which are used in power plants and to propel ships will possibly give way to fusion reactors which will run on cheap, abundant fuel but, as now envisaged, produce unacceptable levels of radiation. Fusion reactors remain a distant prospect.

As has already been pointed out, much of the radioactivity released into the environment has yet to reach the world ocean.

It awaits the whims of the winds, the leaching activity of fresh water and the destruction of containers. Marine organisms are as effective at building up high concentrations of radioactive elements as they are with chemical toxins. Oysters gathered 250 miles from any nuclear source have been found with 200,000 times more radioactive zinc than the surrounding ocean. Measurements made in the Columbia River in the Western United States show how radioactivity accumulates in food chains to reach alarming levels. The river plankton contained concentrations 2,000 times greater than the concentration in the river water, the fish and ducks feeding on the plankton contained concentrations 15,000 and 40,000 times greater, young swallows fed on river insects contained 500,000 times greater, and the radioactivity of the egg yolks of water birds was more than a million times greater. Measurements of the concentrations of radioactive substances in marine phytoplankton show that they tend to concentrate activation products (the solid and liquid wastes from fuel reprocessing plants). Similarly, 88 percent of the radioactivity found in tuna taken from the open sea near the Marshall Islands was due to activation products. One estimate is that 99.9 percent of all radionuclides released by man into the environment comes from fuel reprocessing plants.

The effects of current levels of radioactivity in the marine environment—and the possible effects of projected future levels—have not been studied much. It is known that life on Bikini Atoll is still severely hampered by the tests conducted there in the fifties. The Pacific island's inhabitants have been encouraged to return to the island but are unable to eat their favorite foods. The coconut crab has accumulated such dangerous levels of radioactive strontium that it may never be eaten again. After the tests in Bikini Atoll in March 1956 hundreds of tons of fish caught in the vicinity by Japanese fishermen had to be destroyed.

Experiments have shown that continuous discharge of low-level wastes can cause damage to hereditary material of all kinds of organisms and thereby cause abnormal growth and fatalities. Other experiments show that shellfish and fish can suffer a reduction in their ability to tolerate changes in the temperature and salinity of sea water. This severely restricts their range and suggests that other aspects of their physiology may be affected. It is very difficult, perhaps impossible, to establish what effect low-level radiation has on the populations of entire species. Polikarpov, the Russian scientist mentioned earlier, is worried that adverse effects on the early vulnerable stages of the fish's life could deplete stocks of fish noticeably in a matter of a few years.

The lack of information should not be used as an excuse to pretend that no damage is being done. We do not know what is happening and until we do we should exercise tight control over our activities. Present controls are aimed at making sure that no humans are exposed to excessive levels, and it is disputed by Gofman and Tamplin whether even this is being achieved. Aside from this it is easy to worry that what appears to be safe for man may not be safe for some marine organisms —particularly predators, such as birds, at the tops of food chains. There is an urgent need for the initiation of a worldwide monitoring scheme to determine the levels of radioactivity present in as wide a range of marine species as possible. This should be coupled with a program which attempts to determine the lethal and sublethal effects of long-term exposure to low-level radiation. It might then be possible to assess the effectiveness of existing controls and to formulate any new ones which might be necessary.

Immediate steps should be taken to make some of the less responsive organizations, such as the United States Atomic Energy Commission, more answerable to national and international concern about their activities and their effects on the global environment. There are promising signs that the dumping of containerized high-level wastes will soon be considerably reduced. It would be reassuring if containers already dumped were periodically examined by divers or remotely controlled

TV cameras for signs of corrosion and breakage. The major obstacle to sane controls may well be that the very mentality which has led to the horrific abuse of atomic power for military ends and to the worship of enormous centralist power generation schemes is exactly the sort of mentality that is least susceptible to gentle persuasion and arguments based on subtle considerations of facts about brine shrimps.

The Marginal Seas

9

We have seen how difficult it is to sort out the precise effects of a particular fishery or of the introduction of a particular substance into the marine environment. We have also seen how this can lead to inappropriate controls or be used as an excuse for inaction. It is now time to look at the combined effects of the fisheries and the various substances which have been introduced into the marine environment with so little control. The areas of the world ocean which have been most severely affected are the marginal seas. These are bodies of sea water at the edges of the three main branches of the world ocean which have been partially separated from the main body of the ocean by the adjacent continental land mass or by an island chain. The most critically affected marginal seas are those in heavily industrialized areas. The most striking case is the Baltic Sea.

Of the seven countries which border the Baltic, Sweden has been the one most actively concerned about its decline. Swedish scientists of all disciplines have been trying for many years to understand what is going wrong. For many years attempts have been made to establish a group to develop a systematic model of the Baltic ecosystem, and the aim is far more ambitious than that of any marine ecological program undertaken before. In order to understand the effects of local introductions of pollutants a model has to be built, using computers, to show how the physical and chemical properties of sea water are related to biological phenomena and to the processes of climate and geology. The Swedish government has started to finance the program heavily and a large group of scientists is working full time on the project from a base forty miles south of Stockholm. Cooperation with scientists from the six other Baltic nations is being actively sought but is still rudimentary.

One of the keys to understand the Baltic lies in finding an explanation for the increasing frequency with which it stagnates. Examinations of the bottom sediments of the Baltic show periodic black bands which get closer and closer as one approaches the sediments laid down in the recent past. The black bands represent periods of stagnation in the deep bottom waters of the Baltic. This stagnation has been occurring for some time and is at heart natural. Baltic water is exchanged very slowly through the narrow Kattegat Channel with the water of the North Sea and the Atlantic Ocean beyond that. This ensures that it takes a while before the stagnant deoxygenated water is replaced with fresh oxygen-rich water.

The mechanisms leading to the deoxygenation of the water are complex. The increasing salt content of the water during the present century may have contributed by leading to stratification of the water. The less dense, less salty surface waters are effectively cut off from the increasingly salty deeper waters and, as a result, nutrients released by decomposition of waste and dead organisms on the bottom are not returned to the surface layer where they are needed. Large areas of the surface waters of the Baltic are extremely poor in nutrients and consequently can support little life. At the same time the decomposing bacteria consume the oxygen of the deeper waters until it is almost entirely depleted. After that point has been reached the only organisms left on the bottom are anaerobic bacteria

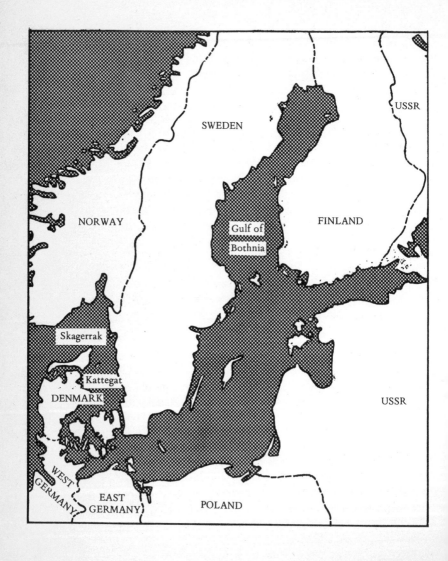

which produce foul-smelling hydrogen sulphide, ammonia and nitrogen gases. The last stagnation period began in 1966 and ended in 1969 when the water was renewed by an inflow through the Kattegat. By the time the new water came, all the deep basins of the Baltic had been deoxygenated and poisoned by hydrogen sulphide. The poisoning was greater than any which preceded it and there are signs that the cycle is about to be repeated once again. The stagnation periods appear to be getting more frequent and the amount of hydrogen sulphide produced is increasing.

The situation is probably due, in part, to the enormous quantities of organic wastes poured into the Baltic by surrounding nations. All seven Baltic nations produced a report in 1970 which showed that enormous quantities of sewage, industrial organic wastes and plant nutrients (especially phosphate detergents and inorganic fertilizers) were being poured continuously into the sea. The bulk of the sewage produced by the 20 million people who live around the Baltic is untreated or only receives primary treatment. The report found that the phosphate content of sewage (principally from detergents) was dangerously high and that none of the existing sewage plants had facilities to remove it. Runoff from agricultural land appears to be contributing an additional large load of nutrients. Heavy blooms of phytoplankton, caused by the nutrients, occur in heavily populated areas such as the vicinities of Helsinki and Stockholm. When these die they add to the sewage and organic pulpmill wastes that litter the bottom. The combined oxygen demand of all these wastes is very considerable and cannot help but exacerbate the delicate oxygen balance in the deep waters.

Another problem associated with the sewage and the widespread decomposition and putrefaction is the presence of bacteria and viruses harmful to man. An epidemic which struck the populace of Stockholm was traced back to a virus in the town's sewage. Other organisms which cause epidemics have also been found. Salmonella survives for a long time and has been found to be present in large quantities in some areas. The bacterium *Clostridium botulinum* has been found in bottom sediments—it is thought to render fish toxic but few fish would be so stupid as to swim around in the stagnant poisoned waters where most of the bacteria are to be found.

Chlorinated hydrocarbons are present in very large amounts and some of the highest concentrations in the world have been found in organisms from the Baltic. DDT residues and the PCBs are the most widespread but the residues of pesticides including dieldrin, aldrin, endrin, chlordane and heptachlor are also present. Fish, fish-eating seals and sea birds from the Baltic have been found to contain concentrations of chlorinated hydrocarbons ten times greater than those in the same species inhabiting Sweden's west coast. There are signs that the level of DDT residues has reached such levels in sea water that the learning abilities of fish are being upset. Migratory fish such as the salmon recognize the home rivers where they breed by the smell of its estuarine water. Sea trout have definitely had their migratory behavior upset and it now seems that the salmon is following the same route to possible extinction.

The 1970 report estimated that 800,000 tons of industrial wastes are poured into the Baltic every year. Most nations take care not to dump much of this in their territorial waters but the end result is still very grim. The sizable pulp industries of Finland, Sweden and the other Baltic countries pour out more than organic wastes. Mercury is one constituent of the effluent which, combined with mercury from other sources, leads Sweden to be one of the first countries to worry about it as an environmental contaminant. Such high levels have been found in cod, herring and other fish that some coastal areas have had to be declared prohibited fishing areas. Pulp-mill liquors have been discovered to be worryingly toxic. They disrupt the life processes of the vital phytoplankton, can taint the flesh of fish and deoxygenate the water. Dumping of other very toxic industrial wastes is being quickly reduced but still continues. It has been calculated that just one dumping of arsenic which occurred some years ago was sufficient to kill the entire population of the world many times over.

Oil pollution is becoming an increasingly serious problem. Spillage occurs frequently and causes much damage to fishing gear as well as affecting fish and other marine life directly. Slicks probably multiply the damage done by the chlorinated hydrocarbons by dissolving them and thereby exposing surface organisms to high levels of the toxins. The problem will be far greater if current oil prospecting in the southern Baltic is at all successful. Just one blowout of one oil well would be an inconceivable disaster in the confines of the already over-stressed Baltic.

There are, as yet, no controls which apply to all nations bordering the Baltic. There is not even a uniformity among the individual controls exercised by each country. This does not reflect differences in the activities of the different countries; it is the result of haphazard planning. It would obviously be advantageous if all seven nations agreed what containerized wastes should be dumped, where they should be dumped, how they should be dumped. Any dumping which does occur should be fully documented and there should be harsh penalties for contravention of any agreement. There should be minimal requirements for the discharge of sewage: even if a community cannot afford full tertiary treatment (though many Baltic communities could) it can be careful in siting sewage outfall pipes and it can make sure that local industries are made responsible for the adequate treatment of their organic wastes. The laws concerning chlorinated hydrocarbons vary considerably but there does seem to be a consensus that their use should be curtailed. The main obstacle to common agreement is the polarization of the countries into east-west camps. So far there have been no regional European agreements about environmental controls that have bridged this gap. The Baltic seems as good a place as any to start.

One of the most worrying thoughts about the Baltic is what would happen if the North Sea's bottom waters were to be deoxygenated. The Baltic would then have no source of renewing oxygen-rich water and would be doomed. There are some Swedish marine biologists who publicly express fears that it may already be too late to reverse the decline of the Baltic— they merely hope to hold the damage at present levels or at least slow the decline. They are saying that attention should be switched, while there is still time, to the Skaggerak and to the North Sea. The Skaggerak is the channel beyond the Kattegat and between Norway and Denmark, and it receives the wastes of Oslo and of the Northern Danish towns. The Norwegian fiords which open into it are naturally stagnant, like the Baltic, and the Skaggerak is showing signs that it might be in the early stages of a decline similar to that of the Baltic. Both the Norwegian and Danish governments are concerned and research is currently in progress to determine the extent of the problem.

Professor Otto Kinne, director of a large marine biology research station on the North Sea island of Heligoland, has aptly described the North Sea as "the industrial cesspool of Europe" and warned that "we know too little to make any safe predictions about the effects of this pollution on marine life." The coast has been the first area of the North Sea to register the effects in ways that have been noticeable to man. The populations of all the coastal marine birds have been declining drastically, and this is thought to be largely due to reproductive failures resulting from residues of chlorinated hydrocarbons and to oil slicks which coat the birds. Another important factor is man's encroachment on the coastal habitat. Industrialization and amenity uses of the coast are taking their toll of wild life. If, as seems probable, London builds its third airport on mudflats in the Thames estuary, then a whole species could be driven from Europe forever. The Brent goose winters here in vast numbers and will be unable to coexist with an airport. Planners are unlikely to be deeply moved by this probability. Smaller decisions than this are being taken all round the North Sea and the total impact is sad to behold.

The rivers which drain into the North Sea are among the

dirtiest in the world—indeed the Rhine might well be the dirtiest. In Belgium, around Ghent and Antwerp, the rivers have been found to be so dirty that even industry finds the water unusable. Britain has had some small success in cleaning up its rivers but it still has a long way to go. The Tyne, which pours out of Northeasten England into the North Sea, will take a long time to become anything like clean. Some parts of its river bed consist of thick layers of sediment that have compacted and set like concrete.

There are plans to build forty nuclear reactors along the length of the Rhine in the next few decades. By the time it is discharged into the North Sea the river water will contain high concentrations of low-level wastes and will probably have been raised in temperature considerably. There are already indications that some areas of the North Sea have built up high concentrations of radioactive caesium. The countries along the Rhine seem, at present, totally disinclined to control their discharges into the river, so one can expect much more than radioactive wastes to float down it to the North Sea. The present situation is bad enough: ever since the war the river has acted as an open sewer for industry. Periodically there is a disaster in which an exceptionally toxic chemical is introduced in very large quantities and the majority of the few hardy fish left are killed. The newspapers of half a dozen countries all make a fuss, but this dies down before any official action is taken.

Another multinational threat to the North Sea has yet to be realized. This is the threat of oil. There is no doubt that there is oil under the sea but no one yet knows how much there is or how economic it will be to extract it. It now seems certain that large quantities are involved and that oil wells will be drilling the sea bed within a few years. Norwegian and Scot fishermen are already complaining that the fishing industry will be ruined by the inevitable spillages. This would be a bitter blow to the fishermen of Europe, as they have, up till now, made more than token gestures to conserve their fish stocks. Mesh sizes are controlled so that immature fish are not caught, landings of certain species are limited and there are close seasons for the catching of some species. These constraints were agreed by all the nations involved and are enforced by fishery protection vessels.

There is a good case for the creation of one organization to coordinate the various controls necessary on the many different and often mutually conflicting activities that are carried out in the North Sea. There has been talk for some time of the necessity for land-based controls of marine navigation similar to those used to control air traffic and, as the North Sea is one of the densest areas of sea traffic in the world, it would be appropriate to initiate new controls there. An international body might also be able to promote a large comprehensive program of scientific research parallel to the Swedish Baltic research project. An integral part of this could be a continuous monitoring program which could give warning of problems before it is too late to solve them. Monitoring of oil pollution is already being carried out by a Norwegian boat which regularly crosses the North Sea collecting samples of sea water. Efforts such as this should be added to and coordinated with the collection of other information.

Even the Black Sea, which is bounded for the greater part by just two countries (the Soviet Union and Turkey), has proved difficult to protect from the depradations of industrial man. It is even more sensitive than the Baltic as it is only connected to the rest of the world ocean by a very narrow channel. It is the largest stagnant basin in the world and is thought to have been stagnant for over 6,000 years. The water is exchanged with oxygenated water from the Mediterranean very slowly—it has been calculated that the water spends an average of 1,350 years in the sea before moving out to be exchanged. Industrial wastes and sewage, principally from the Soviet Union, enter the sea in very large amounts. One unusual form of environmental disruption resulted from the release of young fish from the Sea of Japan which were released into the Black Sea by the bilge pumps of ships. Once in the sea, the predatory fish survived well and badly depleted oyster beds near the shore.

Other fisheries have been affected by widespread oil spillages. It was found that large amounts of oil were being carried into the sea by the rivers, much of it originating from factories and workshops, and this has yet to be effectively controlled. An enormous quantity also came from ships and tankers. Until recently there was not one port on the Black Sea with facilities to store oil wastes from ballasting and tank cleaning. Now the port of Shaskharis has these facilities but the rest of the coast has not yet followed suit. The problem of the Black Sea remains a Soviet one. On paper this country has tough anti-pollution laws involving prison sentences. In practice these have been held in abeyance except in instances of strong public concern. The laws on water pollution are much harsher than those of most countries but efforts are being concentrated on the control of bodies of water that are already overabused. Less attention is paid to the black Sea than the Caspian, which is in a shocking condition—many valuable fisheries (such as the sturgeon) have been reduced to a pathetic state.

The Black Sea is an adjunct of the Mediterranean and it is this marginal sea which will possibly be the biggest testing ground of international cooperation in the conservation of marine resources. The Mediterranean is bigger than the other marginal seas mentioned, is bordered by more countries, receives larger quantities of wastes and is a more valuable amenity and food resource. The problems, too, are bigger and more intractable, and once again time seems to be running out. It has been predicted that within three years a three-mile band of water right round the once beautiful coast of the Mediterranean will be a biological desert. Little seems to stand between this dire prediction and reality. Already large stretches of coast are effectively dead.

As with the other marginal seas, the Mediterranean's oxygen balance is delicate. The Mediterranean exchanges water with the Atlantic, but a complete turnover takes eighty years. Oxygen also reaches the deeper Mediterranean water through its three "lungs"— the upper Adriatic Sea, the Aegean Sea and the Provençal Basin off southern France. These three stretches

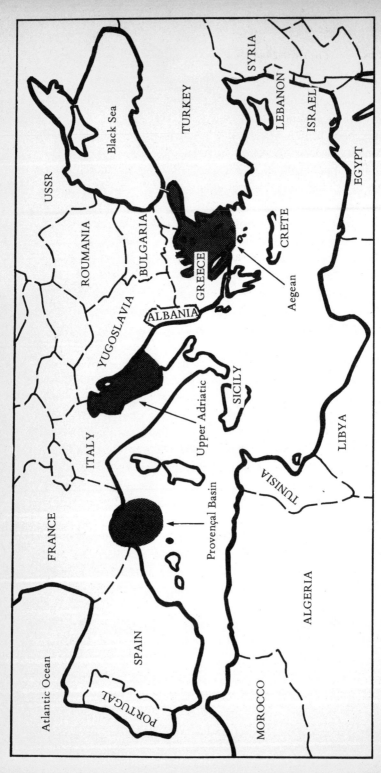

The Mediterranean. The three shaded areas are the sea's 'lungs'.

of water are cooled by cold continental air masses which flow over them, and once cooled they sink, carrying their dissolved oxygen with them. Unfortunately all three of these lungs are in very poor health and no one is too happy about the possible consequences to the rest of the Mediterranean.

The upper Adriatic is probably in the worst state. The number of fish has been drastically reduced, and in the Gulf of Maggia, near Trieste, they have died out completely, leaving the water largely populated by just ten of the most pollution-resistant species. The National Science Research Council of Italy has classified all the bay's beaches as polluted. Bacteria counts on the beaches are high and there is concern that a threat to health may develop. Yugoslav beaches of the upper Adriatic are badly affected by oil and other wastes washed up on the beaches. Synthetic detergents are found to form a continuous surface film in much of the area, which impedes reoxygenation of the water, while the oil that finds its way into the sea also helps to deplete the water of its oxygen. Lord Ritchie-Calder, in a report on the Mediterranean he made to the California Center for the Study of Democratic Institutions, pointed out that one liter of oil depletes 400,000 liters of sea water of its oxygen, and 100,000 tons of oil is thought to be poured into the Mediterranean annually. There is also a backlog of oil which is released slowly. Large numbers of ships were sunk in the sea in the last war and it is thought that as they corrode they are gradually releasing oil. Plankton nets trawled across the surface of the Mediterranean captured tarry lumps of oil in more than 75 percent of the trawls. The combined effect of the cooling winds, oxygen-demanding sewage, synthetic detergents and oil is a marked decrease in the oxygen content of the deeper waters of the Adriatic.

The Aegean Sea is not in such poor condition but shows signs of decline. The only beaches to be extremely badly affected are near Pireaus and Salamis. The Provençal Basin is in as bad a state as the upper Adriatic. The densely populated region around Marseilles has no sewage clearing station; the river Huyenon acts as open sewer for the inhabitants and as a waste disposal system for the factories. It carries its load off to the sea just outside the city. In the summer it is rerouted through an ancient sewer to a point a few miles further away but the winds often blow all the discharged materials right back to the winter dumping grounds. There is a far greater problem sixty miles west of Marseilles in the area of Fos where a new Europort is in operation. The port is large enough to take supertankers and will act as the center of an enormous new industrial complex which will take thirty years to complete. Official projections promise that by 1990 the new center will be producing two-thirds of the present French output of steel, of power and of petroleum products and will employ 250,000 people. Many local politicians are worried that little will be done to control the environmental depredations of these new industries. The oxygen situation of the Provençal Basin is already critical so it would seem that every step ought to be taken to reduce future oxygen loads. The very reverse is happening.

The decline of the Mediterranean expresses itself in more ways than the diminishment of oxygen in its three "lungs". The tourist industry is being hit locally and in one or two years may be seriously threatened right around the Mediterranean coast. It is an enormous industry which brings many people a living and satisfies the recreational needs of millions of Europeans (over 20 million visit the Adriatic alone each year). Despite this the industry itself is lax about sewage disposal and has probably made a large contribution to the wastes that are washed up on the beaches each summer. Every one of Italy's 6,000 registered beaches is dangerously polluted, according to the standards of the Health Ministry. The beaches of Genoa are so polluted that anyone foolhardy enough to use them is advised to get innoculated for tetanus and typhoid before so doing.

Far less is being done to curb the pollution of the Mediterranean than is being done around the Baltic and the North Sea. Within national boundaries little is being done to curb industrial pollution of rivers and waters near the shore. Even less is done to control the tourist industry—to prevent it from cutting its own throat. International cooperation is almost nonexistent. Local politicians in Southern France still solemnly get up and claim that the filth on their electorates' beaches comes from Italy. More energy is devoted to the apportionment of blame than to the investigation of damage and to the prevention of future damage. Oil pollution continues to increase without any concommitant growth in the controls on it. Many new refineries are arising along the coast and few of them have reception facilities for waste oils. Supertanker traffic is increasing all the time. One supertanker disaster in the Mediterranean could release in a short period of time (a week, perhaps) as much oil as is at present thought to be released in the course of a whole year. A very good case could be made for the prohibition of supertankers from marginal seas and other confined bodies of water—especially those with a critical oxygen balance—but it is unlikely that the case would be taken seriously by many governments, most of whom are in no position to argue with multinational oil companies.

The European marginal seas would be considerably helped if the European Economic Community extended its environmental legislation. Much of this has so far been directed at pesticides but there has been talk of tighter controls on synthetic detergents and artificial fertilizers. Such legislation would have to be coordinated with that of East European and North African nations if it were to be entirely effective, although North African nations are at present contributing little in the way of pollution to the Mediterranean. Although it is partly their oil that is being spilled, it is others who are spilling it. On the other hand, they are the ones who will lose most in relation to the little damage done. Their tourist industry could be wrecked before it has a chance to develop. Their fisheries are in decline. In one instance, the decline of the East Mediterranean sardine fishery, it is probable that the damage was not done by the other more industrialized Mediterranean nations; it could be that the damming of the Nile at Aswan has reduced the amount of nutrients flowing into the East Mediterranean enough to deprive the sardine of its food—the phytoplankton which feed on the nutrients.

The heavily populated and industrialized marginal seas of Europe may be the most critically disrupted bodies of sea water on the planet but there are signs that even the marginal seas of less populated, less industrialized areas are beginning to suffer. The islands of the West Indies appear to be creating problems in the Caribbean Sea and to be suffering from them. The small islands have considerable problems disposing of their wastes: their economic resources are very limited and are in sufficient for piped sewage and centralized treatment works. Surprisingly little is known about the rate of breakdown of sewage in tropical environments, and planners take little account of the disposal of wastes in their development programs—a characteristic shared with their colleagues in some industrialized nations.

The situation is aggravated by the incursion of more advanced technologies. When the *Ocean Eagle* disaster occurred in San Juan Harbor, Puerto Rico, the islands did not have the facilities to deal with the ensuing mess. Many important tourist beaches were destroyed overnight. The petrochemical industry has been actively enticed to some of the islands by tax concessions, and this development brings very little employment and causes an enormous amount of destruction to the coast. Some day soon someone will do the sums and notice that more money is being lost by the islands than is being gained by the presence of the petrochemical industry. When that time comes the industry will probably move somewhere else and repeat its performance rather than learn to act responsibly.

Polar and Coral Seas

10

In theory the polar and coral seas are about as different as two marine ecosystems could be. In practice, they have proved to be equally vulnerable to the attentions of man. Neither occurs in areas which are heavily populated or industrialized, yet both are in serious decline brought about by human activities or are threatened with it.

Both are highly productive areas of the world ocean. The 12 million square miles of the circumpolar Antarctic Ocean are richer than any other comparable area of ocean. Very few species are present but each species exists in vast quantities. The richness of the waters is due to enormous upwellings of nutrient-laden currents and to the coldness of the waters.

An experiment with sea urchin eggs back in 1908 showed that a reduction in temperature of 10 degrees increased their length of life a thousand times while the period of development increased by only three times. Because of the increased lifespan and comparatively minor decrease in rate of development, Antarctic organisms reproduce many times before dying and many generations live together. Even the higher vertebrates such as birds and whales are only present as a few species but in large numbers. The food chains tend to be very short as a consequence of this simplification.

The same applies to Arctic life. The short food chains of the Arctic first displayed their vulnerability when measurements were made to determine the environmental consequences of American nuclear tests made above ground level before the Test Ban Treaty. It had been assumed that the fallout pushed up into the upper atmosphere would stay there for a considerable time and that much of it would, therefore, have decayed before finally reaching the ground again. In fact, currents in the upper atmosphere carried the fallout back to the ground in a matter of months and did not disperse it nearly as much as was hoped. The Northern Temperate Zone was the major recipient of this waste but it was found to have made its mark right into the Arctic. Eskimos and Lapps were found to have much more radioactivity in their bodies than people in the Northern Temperate Zone—although the Arctic was only receiving less than 10 percent of the radiation received in the latter zone. The mystery was explained when it was found that lichens were taking in radioactive substances directly from the air, whereas grass and other temperate plants can only absorb them through the soil which can dilute them. Once in the lichen the radioactivity was quickly passed up the short food chains via the lichen-eating caribou and reindeer to man.

Chlorinated hydrocarbons have also been detected in Arctic lichens and plants and in the organisms that feed on them. It is conjectured that lichens may also take these substances straight in from the air and pass them up the short food chains as effectively as they do radioactive substances. Measurements made in the Antarctic show that the equally short marine food chains are also able to build up detectable traces of various substances produced by man. The most disturbing discovery was that the most important element of the marine food chain, the krill, contained residues of chlorinated hydrocarbons. The krill are present in vast quantities in the Antarctic and form the basic foodstuff of most fish and the big mammals (the baleen whale feeds almost exclusively on krill). Higher residues were found in the fatty tissues of fish, whales, seals, penguins and other birds. Penguins and seals were discovered to have, in some cases, concentrations of DDT residues equal to those found in organisms from heavily industrialised areas of the northern hemisphere.

When these findings were first published it is not surprising that they caused more than a little surprise. The realization that man had reached the most remote corners of the planet with his chemical armory was an unpleasant one. The next problem was to explain how they traveled so far, and this problem is still far from completely solved. Research is placing more and more emphasis on the atmosphere rather than rivers as the principal agent in the global transport of chemical pollutants such as the chlorinated hydrocarbons, but even so it is amazing that air currents should carry chemicals so far and so fast and that they should disperse them so widely. It is regrettable that there has yet to be a global monitoring program of chemical pollutants. Until such a program is created we will not know whether the atmospheric concentrations of the Antarctic are greater or less than those of other remote areas of the planet, and we will not be able to track the paths taken by them.

Both the Arctic and Antarctic have suffered from overexploitation of some of their few species. Arctic fish catches started to fall in the early sixties and show little sign of recovering. These are some of the largest fisheries open to human use and could yield far greater catches if rationally managed. The Antarctic fisheries have yet to become large enough to be a problem, though whaling, as was mentioned earlier, has got out of hand and there seems little possibility that the decimated species will ever have the opportunity to recover.

The greatest threats in the future will arise from neither overexploitation nor the presence of pollutants carried in from industrialized areas. It will come from the exploitation of their enormous mineral resources. As was mentioned, huge fields of oil exist not just in Alaska but right round the Arctic. The Rus-

sian government has ambitious plans to tap its Siberian fields
and to pipe a significant fraction of the resultant oil to the Japanese. The continental shelf around the Antarctic continent and
Antarctic island groups has yet to be explored. There have been
many instances of birdkills caused by Arctic oil spills and there
seems to be general agreement that oil will take considerably
longer to break down in the Arctic, that Arctic waters can ill
afford the deoxygenation which oil causes and that Arctic organisms and ecosystems are far more vulnerable to oil damage
than other marine communities. On the other hand, oil resources
are being depleted at a considerable pace elsewhere and few
governments feel like interfering too much with this wonderful
opportunity to grab some more "cheap" fuel. The United
States government has done little to eliminate the dangers in-
herent in the exploitation of Alaskan oil. Neither have the oil
companies involved. The pipes for the Alaskan pipeline have
already been shipped from Japan to Alaska while the government is still officially "considering" whether the pipeline should
be built.

Oil may only be the start of the story. The Arctic contains
many mineral resources other than oil, and once the infra-
structure has been created to remove oil it could equally well be
used for the exploitation of these other resources. The dangers
of disrupting or melting ground in permafrost regions will be
only one of the difficulties. Sewage disposal is a problem which
remains unsolved, and in just one area of the Arctic the U.S.
Navy and other groups under contract for oil exploration have
collected an estimated quarter of a million drums of human
wastes because they could think of no way of disposing of them.
Arctic fresh water and sea water would most probably be severely affected if wastes were dumped in them, since low temperatures slow down the chemical reactions of decomposition considerably. The most disturbing possibility is the release of viruses
and bacteria harmful to man. These could survive for very long
periods of time and wreak havoc in small isolated communities.
The Antarctic continent is safest in that it is still treated as an

international scientific laboratory. It is encouraging that this status has been maintained but one wonders what would happen if valuable, exploitable mineral reserves were discovered on the continent.

The coral seas are already in serious decline, though they are theoretically far more stable than the polar seas. The coral ecosystem has been described as "the most complex and perhaps the most productive biological system in the world." Many also consider it to be the most beautiful. Coral reefs and atolls are much more extensive than one might believe: they cover a total area calculated to be twenty-five times greater than that occupied by the United States. As they are among the most biologically diverse communities they provide a rich and varied diet to local peoples, often in areas where land food is limited in choice and quantity. Scientists have found that the variety of organisms in a coral community is reflected by the variety of pharmacologically active compounds in them. The drug industry is at present examining one of these compounds as a potential birth control agent which could be used the "day after."

Coral communities are always found in shallow waters at or near the surface and are therefore accessible to man and his products. None of the coral reefs or atolls are, however, situated close to the heavily populated, industrialized areas of the world such as are found in the Northern Temperate Zone, and many of them are very remote indeed. For this reason, and because of their complex ecological controls, it might be thought that the coral seas would be among the healthiest on the planet. This is, unfortunately, far from being true. The world's largest coral community, the Great Barrier Reef, is already devastated for part of its length and much of the rest is in decline. By 1969 one Australian airline had already begun to advertise: "Come and see the Great Barrier Reef—before it's too late." Reports from the Red Sea, the Indian Ocean, Hawaii and Florida describe further declines. Commandant Jacques-Yves Cousteau and his close associates have been exploring coral seas for sixteen years, and they have probably got more firsthand experience of these seas than any other men alive today. It is disturbing to learn of the changes they have noticed. In recent voyages they have revisited sites where they first dived many years ago and found that communities which were once thriving are now cemeteries of crumbling dead coral. Cousteau warns that man's assault on the living coral is continuing at an accelerating rate and that "Even at the present rate, in ten years' time the damage will be irreversible."

We are busily destroying coral communities before we have had an opportunity to understand them. The strange population explosion of the crown-of-thorns starfish, for instance, is still a mystery to scientists. Before the sixties this inhabitant of the Great Barrier Reef was a rare animal; little was known about its ecological role, and biologists were happy merely to find a specimen—let alone study it in its natural habitat. When a single specimen was observed in 1960 on a reef outside Cairns, naturalists took boat trips specially to see it. By the mid-sixties the crown-of-thorns starfish was widespread throughout the entire length of the Great Barrier Reef and was found to be feeding upon, and killing, large areas of coral. Hundreds of starfish could now be seen on a few square feet of dying coral. Naturalists now took pains to travel to areas of the Reef where the starfish was not yet present. By the end of the sixties the crown-of-thorns starfish was beginning to invade coral in the Indian and Pacific Oceans. Invasions were reported from Malaysia, Indonesia, New Guinea and many Pacific islands. Scientists still had no idea what had caused the crown-of-thorns starfish to explode in population, whether the explosion would naturally come to an end or how to bring it to an end if natural means did not prevail. The inhabitants of Eastern Australia were worried on economic and financial grounds about the damage being done to the Great Barrier Reef. Their politicians had shown themselves to be fatally slow to respond to the worsening situation.

The build-up in the population of the starfish was not an

overnight affair. It happened gradually over the years, thereby apparently ruling out the possibility that one of the starfish's predators had disappeared. If, as was originally postulated, one of the species of small fish that eats the egg of the starfish had suddenly moved away from the area, then the starfish would have almost immediately built up to its maximum population. Another possibility was that a predatory species had declined slowly rather than suddenly. One candidate was the giant triton which was being removed from the sea for its valuable shell, Another candidate was the painted shrimp. This shrimp is only two inches long but can soon reduce a crown-of-thorns starfish twelve inches long to a pile of pulp. It seemed probable that, once underway, the population build-up was unstoppable, as one of the predators of starfish eggs is the very coral that the adult starfish eat. The starfish were eating one of their principal predators.

Attempts were made to stop the spread of the starfish. Divers tried at first to kill them as they ate the coral, but this was a hopeless task due to the enormous number involved, the starfish's rapid rate of reproduction and its ability to regenerate from single limbs. A further obstacle was the unwillingness of local politicians to commit public funds to the fight. They were carefully exploiting the fact that the biologists researching the mystery were uncertain as to its causes. They claimed, without any evidence to support them, that the population explosion was a natural cyclical phenomenon and should be left to take its course as natural processes would eventually lead to a downturn in the population. These politicians had obviously failed to read the Final Report to the U.S. Department of the Interior by teams which have been investigating the starfish's invasion of coral communities in the Pacific islands. The Report contains this disdainful passage:

> Some observers who did not participate in the survey advised, 'Let Nature take its course,' or 'It's a natural phenomenon and doesn't need control' and 'Let's study it for a while.' The Trust Territory field teams interpreted all available evi-

dence to indicate that the extensive *Acanthaster planci* (crown-of-thorns starfish) predation is not a natural phenomenon; it appears to be man-induced, and 'Nature's course' would be no more desirable here than in an uncontrolled forest fire . . .

The same report contained evidence that similar population explosions had not occurred in the past. While the politicians publicly indulged their wishful thinking the starfish continued to double in population each year.

The starfish was only the first sign that all was not well with the coral reefs and atolls of Australia and the Pacific and Indian Oceans. Other organisms started to multiply mysteriously. The natural controls of this complex system had been breeched by man and there seemed to be little he could do about it. As he knows such a small amount about the functioning of a healthy coral reef or atoll he is not yet in a position to apply his own precise controls. He can only attempt to curb those of his activities which he has reason to suspect might be implicated in the decline.

One obviously bad practice is the removal of coral for tourist souvenirs and building materials. The former is a selective process which can cause rarer beautiful species to be removed from a wide area: the latter can cause the total destruction of a reef, but is usually limited to a small area. Neither is at present a significant contributor to the destruction of coral life. It is, as usual, what man puts into the seas that is doing the harm.

Dredging has been a cause of considerable damage to the Great Barrier Reef and to the reefs off the coast of Florida. This activity releases large quantities of silt which are borne on ocean currents to the coral. The silt can kill coral by smothering it and it can slow down the photosynthesis of microscopic plants upon which the coral is closely dependent. Sewage can produce the same effects as silt distributed by dredging operations, and the reefs off the coast of Hawaii have been badly affected by the discharge of raw sewage into sea water. The city of Honolulu pumps 40 million gallons of raw sewage into the sea every day. The volume reaching the sea will soon have to be reduced as otherwise the profitable tourist beaches will have to be closed. Plans for a sewage treatment plant have existed since 1932 but action has still to be taken. The sewage depletes the waters of oxygen as well as smothering the coral, and investigations have shown serious declines in coral populations exposed regularly to sewage. Some sewage is also discharged by passing boats. This has been found to be a problem to coral in the remotest areas. Red Sea reefs have been found to be covered in sewage and other garbage from ships. There is not a single port in the world with facilities for connecting up boat sewage systems to the port's sewage system, and until there are such facilities (and the Bermudan government is the only one with plans to create them) boats will continue to discharge their sewage at sea.

Although coral reefs and atolls are mostly situated far away from industrial societies, they are frequently affected by industrialized agricultural processes carried out on neighboring coasts. Soil erosion is a major problem in the tropics, due to the structure of the soil, the strength of the rain when it falls and the nature of the agricultural practices employed; and the cane industry of Eastern Australia and Hawaii and other coral coasts has been associated with considerable soil deterioration. Measurements made in a Hawaiian bay after a severe rainstorm showed that the ten streams entering the bay had carried in enough soil in twenty-four hours to coat the forty-one square kilometers of the bay's bottom with about one kilogram per square meter if evenly spread. The Great Barrier Reef is further threatened by the attempts of cane farmers to compensate for soil washed out to sea. They apply lime in vast quantities to their soil and have noted that corals are limestone-forming organisms. Consequently attempts have been made to gain a license to mine limestone from the reef, and although these attempts have so far been successfully thwarted, the matter is far from settled.

Limestone is far from being the only mineral resource of the Great Barrier Reef. Independent surveys carried out by Japanese and American mining companies indicate that oil, natural gas, siliceous sands, heavy mineral sands, tin and phosphate all exist in sufficient quantities for commercial exploitation to be viable.

Oil is already an agent causing much harm to the Great Barrier Reef and to other coral communities. It does most harm when deposited on corals exposed to the air between tides. Experiments have demonstrated that coral tissue is entirely killed when oil adheres to its surface and that no subsequent recolonization takes place. Corals that are always, or most of the time, submerged under water are not affected so drastically but it certainly does them no good. Corals and the other organisms associated with them probably experience many of the sublethal effects demonstrated in specimens from temperate waters. The phytoplankton are probably badly affected—if only by the increased turbidity of the water.

The Australian government has leased oil rights for the Reef to American and Japanese oil companies but has been forced to stop their explorations because of public outrage. Public opinion polls suggested that 91 percent of the people of Queensland were opposed to reef drilling. Local amenity groups campaigned very actively and received a lot of attention from the media. Their victory, like that against proposals to mine limestone, is not a permanent one. The government has appointed a commission to investigate the possibility of oil spillage during exploration and production drilling and the damage that such activities could do the reef. It is by no means certain that the commission will recommend against exploration. The danger of oil spills was reduced in 1971 when the Inter-Governmental Maritime Consultative Organization (IMCO) unanimously agreed to extend the limits for the discharge of oil off the East Australian coast. Hitherto it had been permitted beyond a fifty-mile limit but this left the reef unduly exposed so the limits were extended to a "safe" distance beyond.

Coral communities can only tolerate a very narrow range of water temperature, and they are therefore sensitive to the dis-

charge of hot water from power plants and other industrial installations. It was for this reason that conservationists managed
to prevent the Florida Power and Light Company from quad-
rupling their discharge of hot water into Biscayne Bay. Their
studies showed that, even under normal conditions, the growth
of the animals and plants of coral reefs can be halted on unusually hot days. Other studies have shown that corals die if
exposed to temperatures 3 degrees centigrade higher than the
maximum temperatures they would otherwise experience.

As there are no species of fish present in large numbers in
coral communities, fishing is mainly restricted to the small-
scale capture of fish that are specially desirable for eating or
sport; sports fishing is big business off the Great Barrier Reef
and the Florida Coast. Catches have been falling recently. In
this case overfishing has probably been made considerably more
damaging by the many other deleterous agents acting on the
coral. In addition to the stresses previously mentioned, pesticides
and fertilizers from the precarious agriculture on land have contributed their own problems, and there are most probably other
important agents at work that we know nothing about.

It is encouraging that the public in Australia and America
has shown such a lot of concern for the coral seas. The United
States government has established two large submarine national
parks off the Florida coast to protect large areas of coral, but
unless similar action is taken off Australia and in the Pacific
and Indian Oceans, these two parks could be the only considerable bodies of coral left in the world ocean in one or two generation's time. The Red Sea corals have earned a temporary
respite because of the closure of the Suez Canal after the six-
day war. It is sad that we cannot develop less drastic protective
measures.

The Pacific and Indian Oceans

11

The Pacific and Indian Oceans cover nearly half the world's surface. They form such a vast unit that it is not surprising that out divisive world has preferred to deal with it bit by bit. The five major industrialized nations of the area (Australia, Canada, Japan, New Zealand and the United States) cooperate to a limited extent by means of their Pacific Basin Economic Council, and this body has approved in principle the formation of an Ocean Pollution Information Center. When this comes into being it will find there is plenty of work to do. Environmental degradation is widespread along the coastal margins of the Pacific basin and has spread to the many island groups dotted across the ocean.

The worst hit areas are the continental shelves of the two biggest industrial states of the Pacific Ocean: the United States and Japan. An indicator of the decline of the marine ecosystem along the west coast of the United States is the rapid disappearance of the predators at the ends of food chains—sea birds are particularly badly hit, and most fish-eating birds are faced with extinction. Pelican colonies were the first to experience near total reproductive failure, followed by colonies of herons, egrets and double-crested cormorants. A colony of fifty cormorants on Anacapa Island failed completely to lay any normal eggs in the breeding season of 1971. Predatory mammals such as the seals and sea otters are also in decline and are frequently washed up onto beaches dead and full of toxic residues. Coastal development is taking its toll of salt marshes and estuaries. Sewage and industrial wastes are pouring out onto breeding grounds of fish and the stocks of adult fish are being zealously chased by the fishermen. Even the deeper waters off the coast are being affected. Deep divers using the submarine *Deep Star* found no life at all below 2,500 feet when they explored the depths off Long Beach, California. Where they would have ordinarily found some of the strange and grotesque fish and other organisms that feed on wastes raining down from above, they found a biological wasteland. The normal ocean bottom sediments were covered in all directions by a thin layer of fine brown material, and the scene was only interrupted by the view of the occasional dead fish or abandoned fish net. Further dives to the south in a completely deserted area brought some surprises. The bottoms of the submarine canyons were covered with heaps of industrial detritus and, as the adjacent land is virtually uninhabited, the material must have been brought there by ocean currents and by boats passing overhead.

The Japanese coast is in a terrible state. This befits a nation which is now becoming aware that its combination of rapidly expanding industry and obstinately finite (some might say small) land mass makes it one of the most polluted nations of the world. Hardly any effective controls on industry existed until very recently and even these are used only sparingly. One of Japan's growing band of environmental activists, Jun Ui, says that "as a country we are doomed. Whatever we do we can't save the situation now. All that Japan can hope to become is a living guinea pig to serve as a terrible example to the rest of the world. At least the underdeveloped countries might learn from our predicament before it is too late for them too." There have been several incidents where large numbers of people have paid for the laxity of Japan's pollution controls with their health and, in too many cases, their lives. There have been more than a few instances in which diseased people suffering the consequences of pollution have committed suicide. There was even one sad case in which a schoolboy, who had not himself been rendered unhealthy by pollution, threw himself in front of a train as a protest against his country's failure to curb environmental degradation. Japan's largest federation of trade unions went on strike in October 1970 to hammer the same message home. In other developed countries it is often claimed that the environmental movement is solely the concern of the secure middle classes. This certainly is not the case in Japan. For the Japanese public the environment is an even more emotive subject than it is in North America and Europe. On the one hand, one has a nation traditionally sensitive to its beautiful countryside. On the other hand, one has a nation dedicated to economic expansion and therefore often in direct conflict with the very fabric of its landscape. The confrontation is far more bitter than anywhere else. Aside from the extreme individual acts, there have been many mass confrontations. Annual shareholders' meetings have been stormed by villagers whose relatives have been maimed by company activities. Students have been killed in riots against proposals to build nuclear power plants on Tokyo Bay.

The confrontation has not yet significantly changed the lax attitudes of businessmen and their official watchdogs. This is much deplored, as Japan, like other industrialized nations, is pouring out so much of a wide variety of pollutants into the atmosphere and its surface waters that it is contaminating far more than its own immediate environment. Air-borne pollutants are deposited over distant bodies of sea water as well as those on Japan's continental shelf. River-borne wastes can be carried along submarine canyons beyond the continental shelf, as can sewage and other material discharged directly into the sea. No doubt any effective application of the existing air and water pollution legislation would cause some industrialists to look beyond their country's waters as a sink for their wastes.

The situation on mainland Asia is a little more encouraging as most of the countries have few polluting industries. The Chinese people, who constitute approximately one quarter of the world's population, contribute surprisingly little to the pollution of the Pacific. This is largely the result of their eminently intelligent development program. Thanks to their ideological desire to be as independent of foreign supplies as possible, very little wastage of materials or energy is permitted by the Chinese. This parsimony is accompanied by a program of decentralization and dispersal of population and industry. This is motivated by a mixture of ideology and defense (preparation for a possible nuclear attack) but it has the useful effect of dispersing the impact of the enormous Chinese population on its immediate environment. Even the large cities left over from prerevolutionary days discharge little or no human waste into the rivers flowing through them—it is needed in the surrounding rural communes. The North Korean and North Vietnamese societies share the Chinese attitude to waste and have few centers of dense urban population. They also have few of the cars and other consumer items that are so directly and indirectly harmful in capitalist countries and in socialist countries that aspire to be consumer countries.

South Vietnam is a woeful special case. Its agriculture and industry have been disrupted by years of war and the damage they do never could equal the environmental ravages of war. The United States has sprayed large areas of South Vietnam with herbicides in concentrations ten times greater than those used for agricultural purposes. Aside from the dubious morality of spraying farmland and forest with these chemicals to prevent the "enemy" (often innocent farmers) from obtaining food or cover, this practice is highly objectionable because of the destruction of plant life it has caused. Over one-fifth of South Vietnam's lush forest cover has been destroyed by herbicides such as Agent Orange (otherwise known as 2,4,5-T). It will be many years before the plant life is restored and decades —or even centuries—before animal life is restored. Although the principal direct damage is done to plants, some animals have been found to suffer increases in stillbirths and congenital malformations as a result of exposure to herbicides. The animals suffer ultimately in any event as they cannot exist without vegetation. Much of the South Vietnamese coast consists of mangrove swamp, and this is completely devastated by the spraying of herbicides: one application kills 100 percent of the trees. The swamps are a rich breeding ground for a variety of marine animals. It is not known exactly what effects the removal of mangrove trees has on these animals but it seems that they are, as one might expect, largely undesirable. Visiting American scientists found that the ecosystem was out of balance and that crabs had taken over. They were eating mangrove saplings and thereby further postponing any revival of the swamp.

The rest of mainland Asia is relatively innocent. The Soviet Union, to the north, is very sparsely populated on its eastern seaboard. This is just as well as this country has displayed as little control over the environmentally undesirable effects of its industry as has Japan. It too has impressive legislation to control water pollution but is none too zealous in its application. Malaysia and Singapore, to the south, have their own minor contributions to make to the despoliation of the Pacific. Singapore, in particular, is in a sad state. In the last few years there has been an intensive campaign to minimize the more obvious, visually offensive forms of pollution that are bestowed upon the waters in the vicinity of Singapore. Port workers skim flotsam off the surface of the harbor waters but there is little they can do about what lies underneath. Admirable efforts are made to prevent oil discharges into the harbor: camera-carrying boats patrol the harbor and miscreants are subjected to heavy fines, but they have no jurisdiction over boats in international waters so Singapore's beaches continue to accumulate the discarded wastes of passing ships. All these East Asian countries depend for a large proportion of their animal protein upon marine organisms (mainly fish and shellfish). If they were to destroy this source or to render large parts of it unpalatable (due to contamination by oil residues, heavy metals, chlorinated hydro-carbons and other toxins) they would not have sufficient agricultural land available to replace it with livestock protein (whether pigs, chickens or cows).

The thousands of islands dotted about the Pacific have not managed to escape the bane of environonmental degradation. The crown-of-thorns starfish spread to the coral reefs and atolls of the area soon after it started its invasion of the Great Barrier Reef, and this symptom of ecological imbalance was followed by other similar symptoms. The population of some species of shark crashed suddenly and mysteriously while that of octopuses rose equally suddenly and mysteriously. No one is certain what the next sign will be.

Japanese, American, British and French are busy hopping from island to island chopping down forests without any re-forestation program or apparent regard for the future. This not only leads to resource depletion, it also causes soil to be eroded and washed out to sea where it clouds the clear tropical waters and smothers organisms living on the sea bottom. The Phillipines government has found it necessary to implement strong air and water pollution legislation. Hawaii has only found this necessary recently but should have done so long ago. Poor land management is causing more marine damage than the fouling of coral waters described in the previous chapters. Fishing has been badly affected in areas other than the coral reefs. Fishermen find that sugar plantation pulp kills fish, fouls propellers, clogs up water inlets and forms a malodorous film on the water's surface. Beaches, including the famous Waikiki, have become dangerous as well as unsightly because of wastes discharged into the sea. Eye infections caught from the surf are becoming increasingly common among surfers. Ecological imbalance is endemic. Twenty-four of the seventy species of bird present when Captain Cook landed on Hawaii are now extinct, and twenty-seven of the others are on the verge of extinction. Hawaii has succeeded in destroying more of its indigenous bird life than any other area of the world. Passing ships have assisted the process by discharging oil, sewage and garbage.

Australia's assault on the Great Barrier Reef is its only major act of destruction against the marine environment, though elsewhere around her lengthy coast some damage has been caused by runoff of soil, fertilizers and pesticides. Harbors such as Sydney are hardly in a perfect state but their waters have not yet deteriorated to the extent of those off the eastern coast.

Neighboring New Zealand has an even stronger agricultural base to its economy, and so far its small dispersed population has not done much harm to its surrounding waters, although some municipal authorities have been criticized for discharged untreated sewage too near to public beaches. The human population of 3 million is matched by an animal population which produces wastes equivalent to those produced by about 36 million people, but most of the animal wastes are distributed so widely through the environment that they have yet to do any considerable harm. Oil has been discovered off part of the coast and is likely to be exploited in the near future. Sizable oil fields have also been discovered in Pacific waters around Indonesia, Malaysia and South Vietnam but these are unlikely to be exploited until this area is politically stable.

The Indian Ocean has been spared the attentions of industrialization that Japan and the United States have given to the Pacific Ocean. Nevertheless, the countries bordering it have yet to develop alternatives to the Western pattern of development in the way China has done, and Tanzania is the only country making conscious efforts in this direction. Its progress is slow but important. Its emphasis on rural development could be adopted with much benefit by nearby countries. Zambia has established one or two rural cooperatives but its possession of extensive copper reserves has meant that it has been sucked into more customary industrially based development.

The Mozambique Channel between East Africa and the Malagasy Republic contains many dying coral reefs and atolls. Some oil drilling occurs in the area and passing ships probably discharge yet more oil together with other wastes. The Red Sea was in poor condition until the six-day war, and even with the Suez Canal closed, many reefs have died and the sea cannot be called healthy. The only pocket of pristine health lies in the remote center of the Indian Ocean, but one is loath to make such statements as fate has a grim habit of contradicting them. Should oil be discovered in some of the shallower areas at the center these too will come under assault.

It can be seen that the Pacific and Indian Oceans are becoming less and less hospitable to life throughout large parts of their total area. If this is the case with such an enormous body of water, it is not surprising that lesser seas are finding themselves in bad trouble.

The Atlantic Ocean

12

The Atlantic Ocean is not as large as the Pacific but it still covers one-fifth of the earth's surface. The countries bordering the North Atlantic were the first to industrialize and are densely populated, and for these reasons the Atlantic receives larger quantities of a wider range of pollutants than either of the other two principal branches of the world ocean.

We have seen how the marginal seas which exchange water with the Atlantic (the Baltic, North, Mediterranean and Black Seas) are all in an extremely poor state. The outer continental shelf bordering the Atlantic itself is not much better off. Birds, such as the puffin, which feed exclusively on oceanic organisms are suffering very severe population declines. Unlike closely related birds such as the razorbill and guillemot, the puffin is not often found washed up on shores in spectacular numbers. Nonetheless, some of its breeding colonies have declined from hundreds of thousands of pairs to a mere handful. The razorbill and guillemot population of Britain declined 24 percent in the three years 1967, 1968 and 1969, and this decline was followed by the death of 100,000 of them in the Irish Sea in the year after. A further 50,000 guillemots and 14,000 razorbills disappeared from the cliffs around the sea where they breed.

The fate of the Atlantic salmon illustrates how the international life-style of the living resources of the sea can conflict with the greed of individual nations. Until recently the life cycle of the Atlantic salmon was a mystery. It was known that they were migratory fish which are born and bred in fresh water but migrate each year to an unknown area of the world ocean where they feed. It was thought possible that they had feeding grounds on the beds of Arctic seas. This theory was slowly vindicated off the western coast of Greenland. For years Greenland fishermen had caught the occasional salmon in nets intended for cod and similar fish. The catches never amounted to much (in 1957 the year's catch is not thought to have exceeded two tons) so it was assumed that the fish came from one river in Greenland where the salmon breeds, the Kapisiglit.

This assumption was rudely shattered in the fishing seasons of 1963 and 1964. Both years were such bad cod years that the nationalized Greenland Trading Company (run by the Danish government) was forced to offer twice the price it had hitherto given for salmon. In the resultant bonanza just about every able-bodied Greenlander put out to sea in search of salmon—some even braved the icy waters in rowing-boats. The 1964 catch was, as a result, a staggering 1,400 tons. Clearly an enormous catch such as this could not represent the stock of one Greenland salmon river. Some of the salmon caught had tags attached to their tails and fins, fixed on by European and Canadian scientists attempting to trace the migration patterns of the salmon. The tags showed that the West Greenland fish were in large part émigrés from Canada, England, Scotland, Wales and Ireland. Further research showed that 60 percent of the fish came from Canada, 30 percent from the United Kingdom and 2 percent from Eire. These countries immediately tried to pressurize the Danish government to curb salmon catches in subsequent seasons. The next year was a good cod year so salmon catches slumped again. Unfortunately that same year saw the birth of a potentially far greater threat to the feeding salmon. Two fishing boats, one Faroese and one Norwegian, fishing in international waters to the west of Greenland, caught a fantastic forty tons of salmon between them. Since then a free-for-all has developed. Within a couple of years the total Greenland catch alone equaled at least a third, possibly nearer a half, of the total adult salmon catch of the countries in whose rivers the fish were born. Catches in those countries fell by over a quarter in some seasons.

Naturally the countries involved directed a lot of acrimonious invective at the Danish government. They claimed that they should be the ones to harvest fish born in their waters— that birth location somehow implies ownership. They pointed out that they spend large sums of money conserving their rivers and the salmon in them and that the irresponsible overfishing of Danish boats in Greenland waters was ruining this investment. The Danes could equally well have countered by arguing that, as the fish feed and spend most of their adult life in Greenland waters, they "belong" to Greenland (that is, to the Danish government which administers Greenland). Instead, they chose to argue that there was little evidence that the West Greenland fishery was doing any damage to the river fisheries of the complainant nations. It was the familiar story of a rapist caught in the act and dishonestly cashing in on the feeble state of knowledge of marine biology to justify himself. It was quite obvious that the indiscriminate removal of adult fish from the feeding grounds in large numbers could only be harmful to the entire population of the species. No convincing evidence has ever been produced to suggest that damage is not done. The Danish Government could only have responsibly continued the fishery if it had carried out extensive research into the population dynamics of the Atlantic salmon and determined a sustained yield. Instead, the argument was based on other factors which could be causing the Atlantic salmon to decline. This is an easy task as the species is at present beset by many other problems. A fungus disease causes much damage in some rivers in some seasons: pollution of estuaries confuses the fish's sensory system and prevents it from recognizing by smell the river of its birth; heavy metals, mercury in particular, are toxic to salmon and can kill very young fish. All of these factors should not be used as an excuse for uncontrolled fishing but as a warning that the sustained yield might be even lower than one expected.

Two new feeding grounds of the Atlantic salmon have since been discovered and fished. One, to the west of the Norwegian Lofoten Islands, is eating into the stocks of Norway's salmon rivers with catches of up to 30,000 fish per week. The other, to the north of the Faroe Islands, is dependent on Norwegian, Icelandic and Swedish fish. The feeding grounds of younger salmon have yet to be discovered. When they are the Atlantic salmon could well be brought to extinction. Lord Mountbatten warned some years ago that "The salmon faces extinction long before the end of this century unless something very drastic is done about it." Nothing drastic was done. The charades gone through to implement controls bear some similarity to those involved in the control of whaling. Continuous pressure has been brought to bear on the Danish government through the International Commission for the North-West Atlantic Fisheries (ICNAF) but her rate of acceptance has been slower than the decline of the salmon. By the time agreement is reached there will not be much of a fishery to control. At the end of 1970 the Danes did finally accept that some measures might be necessary to stave off the extinction of the Atlantic salmon. Unfortunately the measures discussed are unlikely to be strong enough. There may not be time to go through the lengthy and disheartening process of strengthening them.

(Even the Loch Ness monster is alleged to have been driven to extinction. A Glasgow scientist claims that the creature has been killed off by pollution, though this report is disputed by watchers of the monster who make regular claims to have seen it since the report of its death.)

Controls on ocean dumping in the North Atlantic are tightening up, but very considerable volumes of dangerous toxic wastes have already been dumped and many of these are time bombs waiting to go off when the metal and concrete containers which contain them are corroded and collapse. Their impact, like that of toxic wastes waiting to be leached out of terrestrial reserves into the sea, will not be felt for a few years. No reliable information is available to enable calculations to be made of what will be released where, in what quantities and when. The most worrying indicator that all is not well in the open ocean is the decline of marine phytoplankton in the surface layer. Marine biologists from Edinburgh have been measuring the populations of a dozen species of plankton in the Atlantic for over twenty years. They have discovered that all of them are in steady decline. This is a terrible discovery. It implies that the whole structure of the open ocean ecosystem is in decay. The decline of sea birds is significant but it pales before the decline of plankton. Without plankton there would be no other life in the oceans. Other measurements taken over shorter periods of time of other species of plankton back up the findings of the Edinburgh scientists. It is incredible that man has had any impact on the enormous stretches of the mid-Atlantic until one remembers the presence of oil lumps right across the ocean and the increasing importance attached by scientists to the aerial transport of toxins. These fall with rain and snow and form their greatest concentrations in the very layer occupied by the plankton. It is worrying that so little data is available to assess the decline of the North Atlantic plankton. It is known that plankton populations can fluctuate considerably but this is usually a short-term phenomenon quickly followed by recovery. There are no signs of this in the Atlantic. Current knowledge would suggest that any declines taking place are induced by man. It is worrying that if this is the case it will be exceptionally difficult to slow down the decline. So many factors might be involved that it would be difficult to know where to start controls. It could well be that unknown synergisms and other combinatory effects of known and un-

known pollutants are partly responsible. Until exhaustive research is carried out (and resources are not currently available
for this) we will have to hope that legislation aimed at curbing
damage to other creatures in other places will remove some of
the threat. Thus efforts to reduce oiling of sea birds and human
swimmers might turn out to be more important as a savior of
distant microscopic plants. This is hardly a firm basis for hope
—especially as existing legislation has a disappointing inability,
in many instances, to even achieve its limited immediate aims.

The North American Atlantic coast is in as poor a condition
as the European coast. Once again the rapid decline of many
species of birds is acting as a warning of things to come. In
addition to reproductive failures ascribed to chlorinated hydrocarbons and to oiling, a disturbing new disease is taking its toll
of birds inhabiting the coastal stretches of the Southern United
States. Many widely differing species of sea bird—including
herons, egrets, sandpipers and loons—have been involved.
Many are dying from a mysterious disease which inflames the
intestines and gives the birds bleeding ulcers. The cause, or
causes, of the disease is not yet known, though it is suspected
that a toxic agent swallowed by the birds might be involved.
Some scientists believe that harmful bacteria and viruses discharged with sewage into the sea may be at least a contributory
factor. For years local fishermen (both commercial and ama-
teur) had been warning that fishing was dropping off, with
fewer species being caught in smaller numbers. The fall in population of local sea birds is a further reminder that all is not
well.

Much of the coast is not rocky and its flat sandy and marshy
margins are vulnerable to any efforts made by man to "develop"
them. Breakwater wars have broken out along some stretches of
coast. Just as whaling demonstrates excellently the self-defeating
nature of killing the goose that lays the golden eggs, so breakwater wars demonstrate the follies of untrammeled competitive-
ness. Breakwater wars start when a property owner decides
that he does not want the sea adjacent to his property to be

eroded or silted up. He builds a breakwater which is designed to stop currents running along the shore from carrying away or bringing in deposits of silt. This would be fine if there were no people up or down the coast from the breakwater builder. Usually there are plenty of people on both sides and they find that the solution of their neighbor's problem creates a problem for them. Successful prevention of erosion by a breakwater may increase erosion on its other side—so the property owner on that side builds a breakwater and passes the problem along. This process continues until everyone along a stretch of sandy coast has built his own breakwater. The next stage is an escalation in the length of breakwaters. The sad fact is that processes of erosion and silting are seldom satisfactorily solved in this fashion: it can result in property being completely eroded by the sea—even houses have been washed away.

Industrial development presents a far bigger problem than private beach engineering. Factories and refineries are springing up right along the Atlantic coast, and reclaimed tidal marshland is often used by industry for the siting of its installations. The state of Connecticut, for example, has lost more than half of its salt marshes. Commercial fisheries have declined markedly in the last few years as a result. The current annual shellfish production is valued at 2 million dollars compared with 48 million dollars in 1900 computed at today's prices. Salt marshes are an integral part of the life cycle of nearly all the marine organisms harvested for U.S. consumption. They are probably involved in the production of 90 percent of the nation's seafood.

The state of Delaware has taken the amazing step of banning new heavy industry along its entire 100-mile-long coastline. In so doing, the state threw away more than 750 million dollars in developments that had already been announced and said no to employment for thousands of people. Few other areas of the world can afford to indulge in such admirable acts. The blocked developments include a 165-million-dollar oil and steel facility on an offshore island and a 200-million-dollar oil refinery for Shell Oil. Shell was reportedly "stunned" at this reversal.

The company even ran into difficulties in a more impoverished area when it tried to establish an oil terminal off the coast of Wales on the other side of the Atlantic. The terminal was to be situated in an area of high unemployment where it was assumed that an influx of money would be welcome. This simple equation failed to take into account the beauty of the coast which would be the site of the terminal. Local amenity groups with limited funds put up a spirited fight and caused lengthy delays in the plans because of planning debates and parliamentary investigations that would not have taken place otherwise. It is a shame that the siting of oil terminals and other decisions about a nation's fuel policy should be resolved by acrimonious confrontations between private companies and local amenity groups. Many of these decisions have such important ramifications that they would even be too big to be taken by national governments.

Refineries are by no means the sole gifts that the oil companies have bestowed upon the Atlantic coast of America. Their product is frequently spilled by passing boats and has even caused problems for islands a fair distance from the mainland. One such is Bermuda. Oil is wrecking her bird life as well as her famous beaches. A government biologist, David Wingate, found that in 1968 oil was clotting the underfeathers of one in every hundred specimens of a bird known as the longtail. In just three years the ratio grew to one in four. As these birds die when oil sticks to their wings and when they eat it when preening their feathers, it is only a matter of time before they become virtually extinct. On the same island the Bermuda cahow, whose population was reduced to a handful by pesticide pollution, appears to be making a slight comeback.

The waters between Cuba and Florida were observed in 1970 to contain large quantities of cellulose fibers. This was initially taken to be the remains of Cuban toilet-paper swept northwards by the Gulf Stream. As Havana pumps an estimated 50 to 100 million gallons of raw sewage into the sea daily this was a plausible explanation. The scientists who made the discovery decided, however, that shipping traveling this busy sea lane was a more likely source. This theory was supported by the discovery of more cellulose fibers in the Gulf of Mexico, which are unlikely to have come from land.

Much of the other wastes found in the gulf may be carried there by the Mississippi River, which carries so much waste that it is considered to endanger aquatic life in the gulf and to be a threat to human health in Southern Louisiana. The Mississippi River system drains 41 percent of the continental United States, so it is not surprising that it should be heavily polluted. The river's discharge is the biggest source of nutrients for life in the gulf but it is also the biggest source of toxins. Thousands of the municipalities in the Mississippi basin have spent hundreds of millions of dollars to treat their sewage before it is pumped into the river, but although this problem is being tackled, others are less readily amenable to control. Industrial pollution is increasing as more industries position themselves on the river to make use of its water, and a very wide range of industrial chemicals is to be found in the river and its life. Heavy metals, especially lead and mercury, are one of the biggest problems. Agricultural runoff of pesticides and fertilizers is also a very severe problem that shows no sign of diminishing. The sugar-cane plantations and other agricultural processes are also losing an enormous amount of soil to the river. The sediment load of the river is probably as significant to life in the Gulf of Mexico as the toxins it carries in. Detailed studies of this have yet to be made.

The South Atlantic is in a rather more fortunate state than the North Atlantic. The exchange of water between the two is a slow, limited process, so the two halves do not intermix significantly. Most of the Latin American and African nations have not had the opportunity to despoil their coast to the extent practiced in richer countries, but their conurbations are increasing in population by as much as twice the rate of their overall population, while piped sewage is still an expensive luxury for large parts of these towns and cities. The product of these two facts is an increasing burden of raw sewage on riverways, lakes and coastal waters. Some of Brazil's beaches have become unusable because of the badly planned discharge of sewage, but the Brazilian government is actively interested in curbing marine pollution. Despite their lack of resources, some of the other South American countries are also taking steps to deal with sewage and other environmental problems.

The only heavily industrialized nation bordering the South Atlantic is South Africa. The diamond-mining industry is a corner stone of the nation's economy, but the yields from sifting gravel and sand on land are falling, and it is now possible to get five times the yield by mining shallow water offshore. Gravel on the bottom is sucked up onto boats where it is screened and sifted, and the tailings left over from the process are poured back into the sea. Studies of other mining and civil engineering operations where large quantities of sand and gravel have been shifted show that the consequences can be unfortunate for marine organisms. The turbidity of the water is greatly increased and photosynthesis is impaired. The bottom-dwelling creatures are completely disrupted. It is probable that the effects of the diamond mining off South Africa are in part undesirable, but it may be asking too much to expect the diamond industry to restrict its activities to the land. The least to be asked is that research be carried out to determine what effects it is having and in the light of this knowledge steps be taken to minimize hazards to marine organisms.

Oil pollution off the Cape is a growing problem, most of it coming from ships forced to travel right round the African continent instead of passing through the Suez Canal. Several tankers have been wrecked off the rocky coast in the frequent storms which characterize the Cape. Sea birds have been badly affected as elsewhere, with cormorants, gannets and penguins suffering the most. The South African government has established a National Foundation for the Conservation of Coastal Birds to save these species from extinction and to conserve breeding colonies of other species. It has also taken steps to protect the fur seal.

Seals are still harvested but there is a strict upper limit so that a good breeding stock is maintained. Surprisingly high chlorinated hydrocarbon residues have been found in dolphins off the Cape, but measurements have yet to be made of the residues in fur seals. High concentrations have been found to have undesirable effects on seals in other parts of the world (for example, off Southern California), but even if high concentrations are found in the South African fur seals there is little that conservation officers will be able to do about it.

The future of the Atlantic is obviously much more precarious in the northern hemisphere than in the southern. The North Atlantic is the most critically affected area of the world ocean and there are signs that nations around it are beginning to realize this. There is still very little legislation to deal directly with marine pollution but the subject is being tackled indirectly by the introduction of strong legislation to curb air pollution and water pollution on land, and, as we have seen, these two channels are of the greatest importance as routes for the introduction of pollutants to the marine environment. There are signs that British rivers, for example, are actually becoming cleaner. Fish have returned to stretches of the River Thames where they have not been seen for years, and a recent government report showed that 76.2 percent of the lengths of English and Welsh nontidal rivers are free from pollution. In 1958 the figure was 72.9 percent. During the same period the lengths of nontidal rivers classified as grossly polluted fell 6.4 percent to 4.3 percent. These figures are encouraging but should not be taken too optimistically. A river which does not display symptoms of "gross pollution" can easily be carrying a wide variety of industrial toxins. The figures for individual pollutants, were they available, could well paint a less rosy picture. Be that as it may, the British government is committed to giving a high priority to public capital expenditure on sewage treatment.

On the continental land mass of Europe it is not so easy to legislate solutions to water pollution problems. About 80 percent of the surface waters cross international boundaries, and the knowledge that, whatever you do, you will never be able to have clean waters because countries around you are polluting the waters which flow into your country is enough to put a brake on water pollution controls. The only viable long-term solution is international agreement. There are various pan-European organizations already in existence that could promote such agreement, but the Council of Europe has tried and failed and so has the International Commission for the Protection of the Rhine. The main obstacle is the apathy of politicians who are worried that the problems of enforcement outweigh the benefits to be derived in the short term. As more rivers become health hazards and as sources of drinking water become dangerously contaminated, this sort of short-sightedness may give way to intelligent action. Meanwhile Europe's rivers will continue to unload their unpleasant burdens into the marginal seas and into the North Atlantic.

Air pollution has also become a subject for international wrangling. The atmosphere, like river water, flows over the entire continent and is not hampered by national boundaries. Scandinavian countries are particularly bitter about the increasing amount of acid sulphurous rain which is falling over their country, and which has had a remarkable impact on fresh-water fish and on the growth of timber. The development of young trout has been impeded in Southern Norway, and vast stands of commercially important timber have virtually ceased to grow because of the rain. The high sulphur content of the rain is thought to be principally produced by the burning of fossil fuels by industrial areas elsewhere in Europe—Britain and Germany are prime suspects though some of the sulphur may be produced by decomposition processes in the Baltic. Detailed studies are being carried out at present, and when the results are published Europeans might find the necessary impetus to create international legislation for both air and water.

The United States has a more promising basis from which to develop legislation. It is largely responsible for its own pollution—as well as a fair proportion of everybody else's. If existing legislation were stringently applied, air and water pollution would be reduced to a fraction overnight. Unfortunately much of it is not enforced. This is sometimes caused by the reluctance of individual states to commit apparent economic suicide by rigorously applying federal legislation to the business organizations within their boundaries. The increasing amenity use of the east coast should provide a useful weapon for politicians pushing through new legislation, but against this the fisherman's lobby does not seem to be very strong in the United States. It is also disenchanted with some aspects of the environment movement, because of the way in which environmentalists lobbied for the closure of some fisheries due to high levels of mercury found in fish. Much U.S. environmental action appears to be sudden and ill-considered. Fast responses are made to issues being given prominent treatment in the media. This process can mean that the views of some affected parties are ignored (fishermen, businessmen and holidaymakers should all be involved in decisions about control of coastal pollution).

The North Atlantic is declining at a far greater rate than any other part of the world ocean of comparable size. We cannot afford to take haphazard action for much longer. If we do not act now we will have to pay later—and not much later at that.

The State of the World Ocean

13

It is difficult to develop an integrated view of the decline of the marine ecosystem. The decline is itself a product of our disintegrated attitude to the environment which supports us, and most of the knowledge we have comes from the investigation of spectacular accidents which have imperiled human health or commercial interests such as fishing. (We were led to discovering the presence of chlorinated hydrocarbons in the phytoplankton of the mid-Atlantic by first finding them in the food we eat.) It is not unreasonable to conjecture that there are substances seriously affecting marine life that have not yet been detected because they do not also commit occasional obvious damage to man. We are still a long way from possessing enough knowledge of the marine environment and of marine life to be able to anticipate the results of our future actions—we do not even know a fraction of the results of our past and present actions.

At the same time we know enough to feel that time is running out. We also know that the interconnections between the world ocean and the atmosphere, which delivers much of the pollutants, make this a global problem requiring a greater degree of international cooperation than exists at present. As we have no appropriate comprehensive knowledge upon which to base such action, we can only make informed (and uninformed) guesses as to the general global pattern of decline and pinpoint critical areas which deserve immediate application of scientific and legislative resources. These critical areas include developments that threaten food supplies and health, parts of the world ocean that are particularly vulnerable, threatened species that are key elements in the maintenance of ecosystemic balance, and sources of dangerous pollutants that appear to be increasing at a much greater rate than controls over them.

Although many pollutants are widely distributed in all three major branches of the world ocean and in many of the marginal seas, there are few that are universally distributed in the same way as salt (sodium chloride). Any drop of sea water taken from anywhere in the world ocean will contain salt. Some of the heavy metals and chlorinated hydrocarbons introduced by man may be approaching this state. Much of the lead found universally distributed in sea water was produced by man. We may have even managed to double the amount of lead to be found in any drop of sea water. Major changes of this order usually take millions of years to happen—thereby giving marine organisms a chance to adapt. Man's changes take only centuries or just a few decades.

Other pollutants are found in locally high concentrations throughout most of the ocean but are far from universally distributed. Oil is largely confined to surface waters, though it is very nearly universally distributed in them. Other substances which enter the ocean from the atmosphere or as a result of direct dumping have similar distributions. Those which enter through rivers are found in fairly high concentrations in estuarine and other sediments and in the shallow waters above the continental shelf. Coastal margins are also affected by human activities which do not add toxic substances to the marine environment but which interfere with the sea as a habitat. Thus New York's solid wastes introduce more sediment to the Atlantic Ocean than all that carried in naturally by the rivers of North America. Other dredging and civil engineering operations cause further disturbances of bottom communities and of the shallow waters. Activities of this nature tend to be concentrated in heavily industrialized coastal areas. Overfishing is less restricted geographically; at present it is mainly a preoccupation of the northern hemisphere, but this is becoming less and less true.

The net effect of these processes has been to cause declines of many sorts in many places. One or two patterns have emerged. The waters of the northern hemisphere are affected to a greater extent than those of the southern hemisphere. Most pollutants are to be found in the surface layer of the ocean and in the shallow waters of coastal margins, the very areas where marine life is richest. The surface layer is also critical to the ecological balance of the ocean as it is the site of the photosynthesis which furnishes the chemical energy vital for the survival of all marine organisms. Shallow coastal waters are equally important as they are the breeding ground and nursery of the majority of marine animals which man feeds upon. Much more attention needs to be focused on factors controlling the population and productivity of phytoplankton. It would be very useful to know exactly how much the turbidity of the atmosphere has increased over the ocean and how much the turbidity of the ocean has itself been increased. The smallest changes in the amount of light reaching the phytoplankton could be doing more damage than millions of tons of pollutants. Attention ought also to be focused on the breeding behavior of fish and on factors inhibiting the development of the vulnerable microscopic early stages in the life of fish and other food animals.

There have already been many cases in which marine food has been so contaminated with toxins that it has been deemed unfit for human consumption. The most vulnerable organisms are filter feeders (such as oysters) which specialize in concentrating some materials by extracting them from the sea water they filter. Unfortunately their selectivity is somewhat limited and does not necessarily correspond to that of humans. The most vulnerable fish are those that eat other fish and are, therefore, at the end of long food chains. However, even plant-eating fish are starting to build up fairly high levels of some contaminants and they may have to be watched in the near future. As time goes by, more and more species from a wider and wider area are affected. Food animals are also deteriorating in physical condition. In the marginal seas and other heavily polluted shallow waters of industrial areas, malformed, diseased fish are becoming increasingly commonplace—as are fish bearing parasites. As these defects do not necessarily endanger health or profit, they have been much neglected hitherto, and this could prove to be an important omission in our knowledge.

Health hazards arising from the discharge of human wastes into the sea have become very great in Europe and North America. Our knowledge of the processes involved is patchy. We appear to know a lot about the pathology of the viruses and bacteria involved but we may have seriously underestimated their ability to survive, breed and travel in the marine environment. Swimming, sun-bathing and other amenity uses of the coast are faced with constraints other than the worsening danger to health. Industrial development of coastal margins conflicts directly with amenity uses by removing coastal areas from the public domain and indirectly by its contribution of oil and other wastes to the flotsam and jetsam deposited on beaches by incoming tides. Population migration to coastal towns causes parallel conflicts. Land is gobbled up for housing, and domestic wastes are liberally discharged into the conveniently situated ocean. Concentrations of population and industry are bound to have a concentrated and locally devastating effect on marine life and on amenity uses of the sea.

All the symptoms of decline previously outlined have been observable in direct, tangible ways, but we could be effecting other more subtle changes with vitally important consequences to man and all life. The temperature of the world ocean in the northern hemisphere rose about 2 degrees centigrade between 1885 and 1940. This rise may be entirely attributable to natural processes; on the other hand, it may be partly or wholly due to human activities. Our burning of fossil fuels may have heated the atmosphere and oceans directly and may have trapped more solar energy in the atmosphere by greatly increasing the carbon dioxide content of the atmosphere. We could also be altering the capacity of the seas to dissolve and store gases such as oxygen and carbon dioxide. Slight changes in these capacities could have a big effect on the composition of the atmosphere and hence on climate and on life. We are certainly promoting the deoxygenation of the deep waters of some marginal seas. We may also be deoxygenating oceanic water by pouring oil into it in large quantities. Professor Lamont C. Cole, who has been active in the recent debates about climatic and other atmospheric consequences of man's activities, reminds us that "There is much that is unknown, uncertain, and controversial about the major biogeochemical processes . . ." Until we know more it might be as well to exercise caution in our interferences with those cycles—many of which take place to a major extent in the world ocean.

Immediate Action

14

Comprehensively planned action is required to
deal with those problems of the marine environment that are already critical and to avert those
that are about to become critical. Any program
created to achieve these ends will need to integrate
the following elements: continuous monitoring of
the distribution of pollutants through the environment and within living organisms; monitoring of
the health of ecosystems; tracking of the paths of
pollutions from source to sink; research into the
individual and combined effects of pollutants on
individual organisms and on ecosystems; devising
realistic enforceable controls. The UNESCO program "Man in the Biosphere" could achieve these
ends if individual governments could be made to
care enough to contribute monetary and scientific resources to the program. There would be a
lot of scope within the program, which started in
1972, for initiatives by independent groups—it
could obviate much of the wasteful duplication
incurred by the current situation where independent groups work without a larger context to refer
to. No separate organization for the control of depradations of the marine environment would be
necessary, though small international organiza-

tions might be established to deal with specific tasks such as the monitoring of the marine environment.

Monitoring was one of the subjects examined by the Study of Critical Environmental Problems (SCEP) in 1970. SCEP was formed in the United States to provide a firmer basis of information for the 1972 United Nations Conference on the Human Environment, and its recommendations for an international program of environmental monitoring are of great interest. It sees the need for a number of advances on the many existing systems monitoring the environment: for instance, one organization should be responsible for collecting data on the pollution of both air and water. There is also a great need for the standardization of measuring equipment and methods and of the data presented as a result of measurements (international coordination of standards is virtually nonexistent at present). Such standardization need not involve large expenditure of money (it might save money by eliminating the collection of irrelevant and unusable information) or the activities of large numbers of people (our knowledge of the carbon dioxide content of the atmosphere is the result of the cooperation of a few small groups of scientists in the United States and Sweden). Continuous monitoring of the environment would be preferable to the existing chaos where the monitoring of mercury in the marine environment did not occur until it had reached such high levels that it was a hazard to people eating marine food.

Monitoring of the marine ecosystem should be of three sorts: physical, chemical and biological. The aim of the monitoring would be to determine what pollutants are entering the marine environment, where they come from, how they enter, how long they stay there, what effect they have on the physical and chemical properties of the marine environment, what biological effect they have on marine organisms. In this way we will be able to spot new pollutants before they build up to a critical level and we will be able to devise more effective ways to deal with existing pollutants. Earlier monitoring of oil in the environment would have forewarned us of the importance of discarded machine oil as a contaminant of aquatic systems—as is it, most attention is focused on accidental oil spillage from tankers which could be described as a marginal issue. Biological monitoring serves as an early warning system. Vulnerable, sensitive and ecologically important organisms (such as phytoplankton and young fish) should be monitored for the presence of pollutants, reductions in population, reductions in productivity, changes in behavior and physiological malfunctioning. Vulnerable marine communities such as those of marginal seas, coral seas, estuaries and continental shelves should be monitored for signs of damage.

One measure of ecological damage is the Species Diversity Index (SDI) which is an expression of the number of different species of organism in a given area and is defined as the total number of species in the community divided by the total number of species in the community divided by the total number of individuals of all species. It is generally true that a system in decay will have a diminishing SDI. Further details of decay can be obtained by observing the populations of "indicator" organisms, A rise in the ratio of decomposer organisms (such as marine worms) would be a sign that a system is probably in decline. None of this data will make much sense without baseline data about the natural state of the marine ecosystem. In order to interpret the significance of a sudden fall in the population of marine phytoplankton it is essential to know how much their population fluctuates normally and to understand the factors which control those fluctuations. SCEP felt there was a particularly strong need for an ocean base-line sampling program. They suggested that an essential precursor to any marine monitoring system would be a one-year sampling program to collect approximately one thousand samples from the following components of the environment: oceans, organisms, rivers, glaciers, rain and sediments. This data would enable scientists to build an outline picture of the passage of pollutants through the marine ecosystem.

There are innumerable oceanic monitoring systems in existence which could, if redeployed and added to, provide a very useful service. Most of them are concerned with fisheries and oceanographic and meteorological observations. Techniques of observation used at present include research boats (making plankton trawls, for example), buoys containing instruments (used in oceanographic and fisheries research), airplanes (used for fish and oil-slick spotting) and satellites (mainly used for meteorological purposes).

Shortage of trained manpower favors the establishment of a remote monitoring system, though such a system would be best suited to the monitoring of physical and chemical phenomena (the collection of most biological data is still largely a pains-taking labor intensive affair). Buoys and satellites are excellent transport media for remote sensing devices, and NASA is launching, in 1972, its first earth resources technology satellite, ERTS-A. This device will completely survey the planet about twenty times in its year of life and will be equipped to receive the different electromagnetic radiations emitted from the earth's surface. It will be equipped with lasers, radar, infrared and panchromatic film so that it will be able to cover a wide range of the electromagnetic spectrum.

The sensitivity will be so great it will be possible, for example, to determine from examination of an infrared film that trees which appear to the naked eye to be healthy are being attacked by a virus. Three hundred and fifty experiments will be carried out by the satellite. They will include the collection of data of importance to oceanographers, climatologists, biologists and geographers. Extensions of this principle could be an invaluable tool in environmental monitoring.

SCEP also specifies eight global environmental problems which it considers to be critical already, and therefore in im-mediate need of monitoring and research. These problems are: the ecological effects of DDT and of other toxic and persistent chlorinated hydrocarbons; ecological effects of mercury and other toxic heavy metals; climatic effects of increasing the carbon dioxide content of the atmosphere; climatic effects of the particle load of the atmosphere; climatic effects of contamination of the troposphere and stratosphere by subsonic and supersonic transport aircraft; ecological effects of petroleum oil in the oceans; ecological and climatic effects of physical and thermal changes at the earth's surface, including changes in land use; ecological effects of nutrients in estuaries, lakes and rivers. All of these involve the world ocean.

It is not enough to collect data. Unless rapid advances are made in theoretical marine biology and oceanography we will be unable to interpret the data we receive. It is all very well to know how many parts per million of beryllium are to be found in oysters off the British coast, but this information is useless if we have no ideas about the metabolism of beryllium in healthy oysters. Automatic devices like the remote sensors which can be used for monitoring cannot ease this problem greatly. The biggest need is for trained research scientists. At present regrettably few scientists are available for useful research of this nature, and the military-industrial complex absorbs a disproportionate number of young scientists who might otherwise engage in this work.

One way to solve the problem would be to use scientists working within the military and industry to do useful work. (A few are already engaged in such work.) They have much of the necessary equipment readily at hand and would earn their organizations some public respect. As it is these very organizations which will have to make the biggest changes when adequate environmental controls are finally developed, it would be as well to involve them as soon as possible. The world's many military organizations have an advanced monitoring system right now. This could be put to much better use if it were used instead (or as well) as a system to monitor the global environment.

A further impetus might come from the establishment of the "adversary science centers" advocated by Gofman and Tamplin —the disenchanted atomic scientists mentioned in a previous chapter. These would act as independent watchdogs, plugging critical gaps in our knowledge which "official" organizations are unwilling or unable to plug for themselves. They obviously haven't much chance of directly influencing legislation but their indirect influence could, through public opinion, be enormous. Centers of this kind are likely to spring up spontaneously in industrialized nations such as the United States, Great Britain, Japan, West Germany, France and Sweden. They are unlikely to fit into any integrated program but they could be an essential adjunct.

Once an adequate theoretical base has been established, and once standardized monitoring data is available, it will be much easier to establish intelligent controls to halt environmental degradation. In our current state of ignorance all we can do is act desperately and negatively. If controls were to arise from a positive program of resource management they would stand a greater chance of being respected. That chance would be further increased if industry and the public were involved in developing the program. Our resources are extraordinarily inefficiently managed at present; competition between different industrial organizations and nations, and the drive to maximize profits, do not seem to aid a rational use of resources. We are beginning to pay for our rashness as we find that our reserves of heavy metals and other raw materials are very close to exhaustion, It is inevitable that resources will have to be managed more intelligently in the future, and it would make sense if that management were linked to plans designed to ensure that the uses to which the resources are put does not damage other living resources.

Scientists concerned about the environment and large industrial organizations are at present tending to polarize into opposing camps. The cavalier fashion in which some large and "respectable" petrochemical companies have ignored scientific advice about the probable toxicity of their products has not endeared them to scientists not in their employ. Nor have the companies enjoyed their courtroom confrontations with scientists helping conservationists to block a multimillion dollar development. The claims of those scientists are often wrongfully dismissed because they are associated with some of the more extreme conservationist stances. The gulf between the two camps can of course be bridged—and is, regularly. Petrochemical companies could help themselves and their society if they aided scientists concerned with the environment to gather the information upon which reasonable controls and management plans can be based.

Even when all the necessary information has been gathered and new, more rational and effective controls have been devised, there remains the problem of enforcement. First of all it is necessary to determine when the controls are being ignored. This function could effectively be part of the continuous monitoring going on. Remote-sensing satellites would be hard pushed to spot a lorry driver dumping drums of cyanide, and even if they did manage this they would not be able to do much about it. Airplanes, which are already being used for spotting oil slicks and tracking the passage of sewage through sea water, might be more useful for detecting contraventions of dumping controls. Once the plane had spotted a dumper a boat could intercept him. There have been instances where planes have spotted oil being discharged from a tanker but been unable to do anything about it because the boat streamed into international waters before it could be intercepted. Integrated controls would remove loopholes of that sort.

Enforcement of controls on the discharge of wastes into the sea would be much easier if there were clear, internationally agreed, standard procedures for disposing of wastes. Discussions on this subject have taken place spasmodically for some years and have borne limited fruit. A start has been made with informal agreements about the containerized discharge of high-level radioactive wastes but there is a long way to go yet. Another aid would be the issuing of licenses for the disposal of wastes. This would ensure that those involved in the disposal were nominally competent and that they were answerable to a controlling body. Highly toxic substances (such as cyanides and radioactive materials) should be licensed from their moment of manufacture right through to the moment of disposal. Licensed operators would lose their license for negligent handling, as well as being subjected to criminal proceedings. Licensed manufacturers would also be obliged to report to a control body the quantities and destinations of the substances they handled. Some large chemical companies are already operating schemes whereby customers who purchase their more toxic products are offered, as part of the purchase price, a cheap disposal service. Once a thorough accountancy scheme is instigated it will become easier for users of toxic substances to dispose of them legitimately and any infringements of controls will be easy to detect.

It is generally easier to control the flow of pollutants into the environments by banning them as near to their original source as possible (it would be highly impractical to demand licensing and thorough accountancy for every substance suspected of contributing to environmental degradation). If the incineration of hearing aids containing mercury is found to be an important source of atmospheric mercury, it might be more effective to constrain the mercury manufacturer rather than the hearing-aid manufacturer. The hearing-aid manufacturer will use batteries that do not contain mercury if mercury ones are not available. It is better that the mercury manufacturer should be made responsible for the subsequent fate of his product, and this also means that one control can stop mercury going to a number of manufacturers making a number of undesirable products.

Even when effective controls are voluntarily observed there will be occasional accidents. We have seen how the crash of one lorry load of phenol in Denmark caused a major disaster and made the Danish government develop plans for a pollution task force to deal with any further accidents. This too could be linked to a monitoring system and could be another productive use of the military. A British scientist, Eric Cowell, has developed a pollution scale intended to give a quick evaluation of the scale of pollution disasters. It would be somewhat similar to the Beaufort wind scale and would help scientists to communicate the relative gravity of different situations to media reporters. His scale contains the following six levels of severity:

I Environmental addition

  (a) Aesthetic damage: view spoilt or place rendered unsightly but no detectable biological damage. (For example, polythene bottles.)

  (b) Possible threat: substance detectable and shown to be a potential biological danger experimentally. Level below that at which biological change can be detected.

II Environmental contaminant: some biological change detectable but not considered to be serious.

III Environmental hazard: organisms at risk. Effect causes concern among ecologists and is sufficient to warrant action to reduce the level in the environment.

IV Environmental pollutant: organisms die and the level of pollution is high enough to merit public concern. The species diversity index of the area is reduced, with consequent loss of ecosystem stability.

  (a) Chronic pollutant: continued low levels result in progressive damage at a rate higher than that of recovery processes. Situation will deteriorate unless measures to improve it are taken. For example, industrial effluents.

  (b) Acute pollution: damage may be sudden and serious but recovery will usually take place naturally. Usually found as a consequence of isolated incidents. For example, localized oil pollution.

V Dangerous pollution: official action is automatic.

  (a) Biological damage: severe, but recovery is possible if action is swift and effective. Mortality will be high, with species threatened over a wide area.

  (b) Radioactivity: mortality may be low initially but species endangered as a result of genetic damage.

VI Catastrophic or disastrous pollution: widespread heavy mortality with little or no hope of rapid recovery. Species may be eliminated locally or even nationally. For example, the aftermath of nuclear, chemical or biological warfare.

One may not agree with the details of the scale but the idea is an interesting one, and a sophisticated version of this scale would be useful for any task force entrusted with the job of dealing with incidents of pollution. Deliberate acts of pollution should be countered by severe economic and business penalties which ensure that the guilty party has no opportunity to repeat his offense. He should pay for any costs incurred by the task force and also pay appropriate compensation to all parties who incur losses because of this act.

The laxity of current legislation and the feebleness with which it is applied may lead one to dismiss possibilities of effective national legislation, let alone internationally coordinated action. Current use of financial and scientific manpower resources into the degradation of the marine environment may seem meager. Nevertheless, I still believe an integrated program is possible. A process of regional multinational coordination of research and control is beginning to gain momentum. Most importantly, public sympathies are changing. People are beginning to place more value on the environment, and opinion polls show that they are starting to be willing to express that concern by monetary sacrifice: they are becoming ready to pay for clean goods.

Increasing public concern will also express itself in direct action. Amenity groups are growing in number and power in many countries, and their role is bound to increase in importance and in the effectiveness with which it is exercised. Their contribution has not always been entirely effective in the past because of the chaotic context of irrational or nonexistent governmental and industrial policies of resource management. Once the responsibility and concern embodied by amenity groups has a more rational framework within which it can operate, industry will find it more difficult to dismiss them as "hysterical environmentalists."

It is a sad fact that the decline of the marginal seas and coastal areas of industrial countries, where most of the controls will have to be affected, is accelerating at an alarming rate.

When there are no safe bathing beaches left and the price of fish shoots up while its availability shoots down, pressures will build up from innumerable quarters. Public outrage will be joined by lobbying from the fishing industry, the chicken and pig-raising industries (who will be reluctant to pay more for fishmeal), the tourist industry and the property industry. At present many governments seem to be more concerned about the marine environment than the citizens of their countries. This will soon change as the information which is worrying governments now is translated into the news stories of the near future. The seas are unlikely to "die" overnight but the scale and frequency of serious pollution incidents is expected by many marine biologists to rise dramatically in the near future. The death throes of the marginal seas will be the biggest and most terrible events so far in the wrecking of our planet.

Long-term Action

15

The program of action outlined in the last chapter can only be a temporary solution to the problem of minimizing man's adverse impact on the marine environment. The world ocean will only be permanently safe from the ravages of man if he implements changes far greater than any which can be brought about by legislation. We are in the process of discovering that the world ocean is only finite—that we are near to overloading it with our wastes and to removing more living creatures from it than it can spare—at the same time as we are discovering that the terrestrial environment is equally finite. We have wrested a large proportion of its accessible resources from the earth and in return overburdened it with the resultant wastes. At the same time our numbers have risen dramatically.

It would, however, be a grave error to imagine that population control alone could alleviate our problems—or that those problems are in large part due to short-term increases in population. Our biggest problem is burgeoning technocracy. In the last few decades there has been a phenomenal growth in technologies that are energy-intensive and produce material incompatible with natural processes. In order to gain energy we have burned up most of our nonrenewable fossil fuel reserves—a process which has added significantly to the carbon dioxide content of the atmosphere—introduced pea-soup and then petrochemical smog to the world and released vast quantities of heat to an environment that probably could do better without it. We have also dug deep into our mineral reserves. Wide-scale environmental damage has been caused by the release of synthetic chemicals into an environment which has not evolved to cope with them.

Scientists at the Massachusetts Institute of Technology have used a computer to project into the future current trends and to see what would happen if we continued to expand our economies, technologies and populations at current rates. Their findings are very disturbing; unless we make dramatic changes civilization will degrade and collapse within a century. The scientists also used their complex model to determine what would happen if various remedies were attempted. They found that population control alone would only avert disaster for a few years. The only strategy they tried which worked when fed through a computer was the achievement of a stable society. The stability referred to is a stability of numbers (where current reproductive rates are slashed so that births just balance deaths) and of resource use.

Our current centralist giant-scale technocracy will have to be decentralized to spread the load. Existing industrial processes are wasteful in many ways other than that in which they gobble up resources: by-products are thrown away; products are made of more material than is necessary; they often require large amounts of energy to manufacture and—once manufactured—require unnecessarily large amounts of energy to operate; they have a short life; the materials of which they are made are rarely reused—in fact energy is used to dispose of them. All this adds up to an amazing amount of wastage which could be avoided—yet we regard this crude technology as "advanced." Any new technology will have to be based on minimal and careful use of our remaining nonrenewable resources combined with greater uses of renewable sources for our energy. We will have to use materials such as wood, natural fabrics, stone and plastics made from seaweed or soya beans. Objects made by using these energy resources and materials will have to be durable, efficient and easy to dispose of—their constituent materials should, preferably, be reused.

Current attitudes regard such ideas as primitive, unsophisticated and retrogressive. Inasmuch as some "primitive" societies cooperate with natural geological, climatic and biological cycles this new technology would indeed be primitive. If the same creative thought which has been applied to the use of fossil fuels and nonrenewable materials were applied to renewable sources of energy and materials we could develop a truly "advanced" technology (we might no longer regard it as a technology but, like eating, as part of our relationship with our environment). Sophisticated solar and wind devices already exist. Like it or not, we appear to be faced with little choice other than to abandon our current greedy and unrealistic habits.

To most people on this planet it would be no big wrench to switch from our current technology to a more sustainable one. The majority of human beings are undernourished, unhealthy, poorly housed and generally badly off. The fruits of our current technology, which are the only grounds ever produced in its defense, are being increasingly unfairly distributed. Any restructuring of our production processes will have to be accompanied by enormous political changes permitting fairer distribution of resources. This would be impossible within our current technological system— we have already passed the point where it is possible for everybody to have electric toothbrushes and so on —but would be moderately easy if self-regenerating natural resources such as wind, sun, trees and seaweed were the basis of society. These resources are widely enough dispersed for central ownership to be patently strange.

Such ideas seem crazily unrealistic now, but as the scenario predicted by the computer unfolds people will start to wonder if the time has not come for change. It is remarkable that, in the short period of a few years, awareness of man's unenviable predicament has spread so far among politicians. American senators, a commissioner of the European Economics Community and the scientific director of the Organization for Economic Cooperation and Development have made startling statements supporting the quickest possible transition from an expansionist economy to an economy of stock, and the taking of other drastic steps to create a stable state society. If action is not taken soon we will pass the point of worrying about the demise of life in the marginal seas and will be faced with the collapse of the Atlantic Ocean and then the Pacific. If events of this magnitude do not destroy man (and most other life) they should finally convince him that the time has come to change.

The world ocean could become one of man's greatest assets if he allowed it to. It contains enough food to feed a large proportion of the present population of the world. It is probably not too late to halt the decline of the ocean. Some scientists have suggested that even if further pollution of the seas were stopped tomorrow there would be such a large quantity of pollutants waiting to be leached off the land and washed out of the skies into the ocean that it would be destroyed in ten years' time. Not enough is known about the situation to affirm or contradict statements of this sort convincingly, but even if the claim proves to have been pessimistic our problems will be far from over. The world ocean will have to be treated with more respect in the future or we will simply repeat the tragedy being enacted at present.

Many things will need to be done. For a start, more care will have to be taken in the selection of animals and plants removed from the ocean, and in this respect a lot could be learned from Eskimos and other societies that have in the past depended on the sea for food. The Eskimos did not concentrate their hunting on one or two species from one or two localities; they removed small numbers of a wide range of species from the entire length of the food chain and from many different habitats.

Then, once the organisms have been removed from the water they should be distributed to those who need them and wastage be minimized. The use of fish as fertilizer or animal feed will have to be abandoned. A close watch on the health of marine communities will have to be made to ensure that no damage is done by our collecting. Sea farming could be practiced extensively on coastal margins in both sea water and brackish water, with the chance of reaching extremely high productivity of protein. Beds of seaweed could also be cultured. Many marine organisms have uses compatible with the new technology outlined before. The wastes of food organisms (for instance, the bones of fish and marine mammals) often have uses to which they could be put. Seaweeds can be used as raw material for the production of alginate plastics, pharmaceuticals, fertilizers and insulation blocks for building. The current practice of regarding the open oceans as common territory belonging to no one nation or group of people should be extended to the entire world ocean. The principle is much abused at present but is intrinsically useful. There is already talk in the United Nations and other international organizations of strengthening it, for, although the current practice of individual nations establishing fishing limits has in some cases saved the stocks of fish, it is a dangerous tendency which could deprive those who need fish of the opportunity of catching it.

There has been talk for many years about the exploitation of the mineral wealth of the seas. The fact that it has fortunately failed to occur on a big scale has saved the ocean from unthinking disturbance and left large quantities of minerals lying around. These might serve as a source for the few nonrenewable resources a new technology would require. Manganese is there for the taking—in the form of nodules strewn about on the ocean floor. Collecting these nodules makes no sense in our present capital-intensive economy, but another society with labor to spare might feel differently. Great care would have to be taken to ensure that the removal of minerals would not affect the more important living resources of the sea.

Planning for the long-term future of the world ocean and its resources is more than a little premature, given its present circumstances. We have already knocked a serious dent in the stability of the marine ecosystem, but possess far too little knowledge to be at all certain how much damage we have done. It has often been the case that when we have assumed the worst about some aspect of marine pollution that assumption has proved to be a tragic underestimation. Should the damage not prove lethal, man will be able to benefit significantly from the ocean. A healthy lovingly harvested sea could yield far more than the rapacious, mindless pillage that we practice at present. It might even yield a little peace of mind. Running throughout man's history there is a deep strand of mysterious attachment in the waters of the ocean. While we maltreat those waters we cannot be at ease. The seas must not die.

Appendix: What You Can Do

Marine pollution and the overexploitation of marine resources have in the past received more attention from concerned governments and intergovernmental organizations than from the public. This situation, which is unusual in environmental affairs, is probably due to the complexity and inaccessibility of relevant information and to competition for attention from more immediate and obvious threats. An issue such as the control of noxious emissions in the exhaust of cars is relentlessly publicized by the media while an apparently more abstruse story such as the effect of lead on marine organisms is sadly neglected. The gap in awareness between the public and its elected (or, in some cases, nonelected) officials is rapidly narrowing as new stories about the decline of the seas come in thicker and faster. This gap is unhealthy for a variety of reasons and should not be allowed to persist one minute longer than necessary.

Action by individuals and groups of citizens can be based on many forms of involvement: as actual or potential consumers of seafoods and of products dependent on seafoods (pet foods made from whale meat, for example, or fish and bacon from pigs fed on fishmeal); as workers involved in processes leading, directly or indirectly, to marine pollution or overexploitation of a living resource of the seas; as inhabitants of houses which pollute the air and water (and hence the seas); as holidaymakers, sports fishermen and sailing enthusiasts; as students with the time and facilities to study global and local implications of the decline of the marine ecosystem and to suggest strategies for halting or reversing it; as voters in local and national elections; as sources of political power of other varieties.

All these forms of involvement form the basis of action. Consumers can mobilize to prevent the sale of undesirable goods. By simultaneously boycotting the purchase of a product, picketing retail outlets and campaigning to persuade the manufacturer to stop manufacturing it, one can knock a significant dent in the sales of that product. Such action can also be combined with attempts to influence local and national legislation so that any victories won become semi-permanent. A complete campaign of this sort was successfully fought in the United States against synthetic detergents with a high phosphate content. Similar attempts could be made to make whaling uneconomic. Sales of petfoods containing whalemeat have ground to a halt in the United States but are still considerable in Great Britain and other European nations. Another important form of consumer action, unparalleled by any previous environmental action, would be a campaign against wasteful and inequitable uses of the living resources of the sea. Bacon manufacturers should be dissuaded from using enormous quantities of fishmeal to feed their pigs. Such actions would of course diminish the economic revenue of developing countries if it were taken in isolation. It must be demonstrated that any situation in which such countries are forced to wastefully overexploit and export protein resources desperately needed for internal consumption is iniquitous and must be stopped.

In the developed countries environmental action is mistakenly associated with the middle classes. It is frequently claimed that the working classes are more preoccupied with personal wealth than with a healthy environment. This seems to be a representation of the wishful thinking of the media rather than an accurate statement of fact. Trade-union movements in many countries have taken considerable steps to curtail the pollution of their work environment as well as that of the communities in which their members live. In Japan national action by labor organizations to diminish pollution by industry has had considerable success. It is often the poorer segments of society who traditionally spend their holidays along the coastline of their own country—this gives them a strong incentive to promote national controls on marine pollution. Workers are also in a good position to prevent overexploitation of the living resources of the sea. It might appear to be a complete fantasy to expect fishermen to promote controls on overfishing, but recently there have been signs that the fantasy is about to become reality. British trawlermen surprised those who remembered the "cod wars" of the fifties by proclaiming that they were not totally dismayed by Iceland's latest efforts to extend her fishing limits to fifty miles. This would deny many waters rich in fish to the boats of Britain and other nations, but, they pointed out, it might also protect stocks of fish and thereby aid fishing in other areas.

Fishing has always been a skilled and dangerous activity; its death rate is only matched by that of the mining industry. Its safety is only improving very slowly and the gap between working conditions on a fishingboat and conditions in a factory on land is getting wider and wider. Once a fisherman has acquired the skills of his trade he is unlikely to switch trades. The men who invest capital in the fishing industry are in an entirely different situation—if overexploitation destroys the goose that lays the golden eggs, most of them are able to reinvest their capital in another goose. There is, therefore, a conflict between the commitments of the fisherman and those who capitalize his industry. The industry is at present overcapitalized and the pressure for a quick return on investments is even greater than it might be. This pressure could lead to a confrontation with fishermen expecting to use their skills for a long period, for the rest of their working lives. If fishermen come to adopt this stance they could exert as powerful an influence on the industries of the sea as the mineworkers do on land.

Householders do not usually consider themselves to be actors in the drama of marine pollution, yet their contribution is far from insignificant. They consume large quantities of electricity and are thereby party to the air pollution which almost invariably accompanies the generation of power. They produce sewage which often pollutes surface waters, and ultimately the sea. When they (perhaps I should say "we") heat their house by nonelectric means they often do so in a way which entails air pollution. Use of private cars and some forms of public transport can contribute further to air pollution. What goes up must come down; what goes up into the air has a regrettable habit of coming down over the oceans. The problems of a householder can in many instances be resolved by concerted local action. If such action is to be successful it must do much more than denigrate current practices and blindly block any new delelopments. Common-sense alternatives must be proposed.

It is far better to launch a positive campaign to improve current practice than to launch an entirely negative one principally involved in bemoaning the loss of the status quo. There are many improvements which could be made to the existing patterns of power generation, sewage treatment and domestic heating. Many local authorities are too overworked to investigate these without public inducement and support. They need to be convinced that environmentally sound projects can also make economic sense and win votes. A solution to one problem can even involve the solution of another. The use of Total Energy Systems (which use the waste heat produced in the production of power) improves the efficiency with which power is produced, eliminates thermal pollution and provides cheap domestic heating and hot-water supply (while reducing the pollution load of these processes).

Political power can also be exercised at a national and international level. The most effective action which could be taken on these levels would probably have to be a part of the action taken by organizations concerned with pollution as a whole rather than with marine pollution. Tough campaigning against air pollution and the pollution of surface waters is every bit as important to the seas as action against direct dumping of oil and other substances into the oceans. Anyone wishing to achieve rapid results would probably do best to join an existing organization which has already established ways of influencing the decisions of governments and of groups of governments. If the organization proves to be unaware of many aspects of marine pollution it can always be educated. If it refuses to be educated and other national organizations prove equally intransigent then there would be good reason to attempt to form a new organization. Even in such an instance it might be better to form an organization generally involved in all aspects of environmental decline rather than to form one specializing in the marine environment. Specialist groups are better formed for specific tasks such as the protection of a particular stretch of beach or the influencing of one unit of local government or as a channel for the talents of a small group (one or two groups of marine biologists exist—they tend to be devoted to the dissemination and exchange of useful information and there is little the general public can do to aid them directly).

Most of the action so far is concerned with stop-gap measures to alleviate immediate pressures on the marine environment. This can only form a part of any long-term solution. Far more radical changes will be necessary but these are beyond the scope of this book.

Bibliography

BOOKS

Bardach, John: *Harvest of the Sea* (London, Allen & Unwin Ltd., 1969)

Clare, Patricia: *The Struggle for the Great Barrier Reef* (London, Collins, 1971)

Commoner, Barry: *The Closing Circle* (New York, Knopf, 1971)

Cousteau, Jacques-Yves, with Philippe Diole: *Life and Death in a Coral Sea* (London, Cassel, 1971)

David Davies Memorial Institute of International Studies: *Water Pollution as a World Problem* (London, Europa Publications, 1971)

Eltringham, S.K.: *Life in Mud and Sand* (London, English University Press, 1971)

Ericson, David B., and Goesta Wollin: *The Everchanging Sea* (London, Paladin, 1971)

Friedrich, H.: *Marine Biology* (London, Sidgwick & Jackson, 1969)

Green, J.: *A Biology of Crustacea* (London, Witherby, 1961)

Gross, M.G.: *Oceanography* (Columbus, Ohio, Merrill, 1971)

Hardy, Alister:
The Open Sea, the world of plankton (London, Collins, 1959)

The Open Sea, Fish and Fisheries (London, Collins, 1959)

Hood, Donald W. (editor): *Impingement of Man on the Oceans* (New York, Wiley-Interscience, 1971)

Hussain, Farooq: *Living Underwater* (London, Studio Vista, 1971)

Iversen, E.S.: *Farming the Edge of the Sea* (London, Fishing News, 1968)

Loftas, Tony: *The Last Resource* (London, Hamish Hamilton, 1969)

Marx, Wesley:
The Frail Ocean (New York, Ballantine, 1969)
Oilspill (San Francisco and New York, Sierra Club, 1972)

Matthews, William H., F.E. Smith and E.D. Goldberg: *Man's Impact on Terrestrial and Oceanic Ecosytems* (Cambridge, Mass., MIT Press, 1971)

Mellanby, Kenneth: *Pesticides and Pollution* (London, Collins, 1967)

Polikarpov, G.G.: *Radioecology of Aquatic Organisms* (Amsterdam, North-Holland, 1966)

Russell-Hunter, W.D.: *Aquatic Productivity* (New York, Macmillan Co., 1970)

Study of Critical Environmental Problems (SCEP): *Man's Impact on the Global Environment* (Cambridge, Mass., MIT Press, 1971)

Sibthorp, M.M.: *Oceanic Pollution, a survey and some suggestions* (London, David Davies Memorial Institute, 1969)

Singer, S.F. (editor): *Global Effects of Environmental Pollution* (Dordrecht, Reidel, 1970)

Study of Man's Impact on Climate (SMIC): *Inadvertent Climate Modification* (Cambridge, Mass., MIT Press, 1971)

Sverdrup, Fleming and Johnston: *Oceans, Their Physics, Chemistry and General Biology* (New York, Prentice-Hall, 1942)

Tait, R.V.: *Elements of Marine Ecology* (London, Butterworth, 1968)

Teal, John and Mildred: *Life and Death of the Salt Marsh* (New

York, Ballantine, 1969)

Walker, Colin: *Environmental Pollution by Chemicals* (London, Hutchinson Educational, 1971)

MAGAZINES

The Ecologist: published monthly by Ecosystems, London.

Environment: 10 issues per year. Published by the Committee for Environmental Information, St. Louis.

Marine Pollution Bulletin: published monthly by Macmillan, London.

Ocean Living: 10 issues per year. Published by William Taylor, Los Angeles.

Index